Women's
Fast Pitch
Softball

Women's
Fast Pitch
Softball

Best of the Best

By
Bill Plummer III &
Steven Clarfield, Ph.D.

Preface by
Coach Mike Candrea

Foreword by
Dr. Dot Richardson

Clear Vision Publishing, Inc.
Manalapan, New Jersey

PUBLISHED BY CLEAR VISION PUBLISHING, INC.
301 HIGHWAY 9 SOUTH,
MANALAPAN, NEW JERSEY 07726

COPYRIGHT © 2012 BY BILL PLUMMER III &
STEVEN CLARFIELD, PH.D.

ISBN: 978-1-4675-0003-6

PRODUCED BY WWW.BOOKSPRINTEDHERE.COM
MANAHAWKIN PRINTING
PRINTED IN THE UNITED STATES OF AMERICA
****

Volume discounts & fundraising discounts
are available. Please contact Bill Miller
at 908-510-8644.

From Bill

*This book is dedicated in loving
memory of Ann D. Plummer,
December 30, 1915 – June 17, 2011.*

From Steve

*To Ingrid, for all the innings
you cheered through.*

TABLE OF CONTENTS

Preface by Coach Mike Candrea ix
Foreword by Dot Richardson MD xi

Introduction: Best of the Best xvii

Part I

Modern Era Athletes

Part II

Experts, Authorities, Coaches & Players

PREFACE

BY COACH MIKE CANDREA

Softball, as we know it today, can be traced to a foundation that has been built one season at a time by very special teams, players, and coaches who have a common passion and love for a simple game played with a bat, ball, and glove. A very special game played on a perfectly-formed diamond! We all know how special diamonds can be in celebrating lifetime achievements and special relationships.

The opportunity to say that you have been personally touched by the history of your sport does not appear often through a career in sports. I have been blessed to have had the opportunity to be touched in so many ways by every one of the tremendous individuals highlighted in this great historical book – a book that tells, with clarity, simplicity and inspiration, the story of the people who have paved the way for the game we all enjoy today! I have learned something new about almost every person discussed here, and reading these stories allowed me to recall some wonderful experiences throughout my career. I admire the common thread of a strong commitment to excellence and competitive spirit. Most of all, I admire their continued involvement and strong desire to give back to the sport we all love.

Thank you for this outstanding book, which will give the reader an opportunity to gain a valuable historical and philosophical perspective while enjoying tremendous insight and background into the great pioneers of softball who have had an impact on our game. This book is a great resource that not only honors the faces of our game, but gives outstanding stories that will help teach improvement in the game of softball and life!

FOREWORD

BY DOT RICHARDSON M.D.

Out in the Woods
Carved in a Tree
Are two little Words
"Remember Me"

Sometimes in our thick forest of daily living, we often don't take the time to recognize those who have paved the way for us and others. I would like to encourage you to take the time, because you might just be amazed at how much one can learn from the *Best of the Best*.

It's said that "true greatness should never go unrecognized." Unfortunately, in the sport of fast pitch softball so much greatness has been overlooked until now. *Women's Fast Pitch Softball – Best of the Best* demonstrates the evolution of the sport through the collegiate ranks and the impact certain players have had on the game. In doing so, the book ultimately captures the essence of what makes these female athletes so great. As you read about each legend in the game, you find yourself drifting back into the great moments of their careers. You can see them compete and hear their examples of inspiration. You find that there are similar ingredients in each one that raised them to the top of the mountain in the sport. You clearly recognize that it is a sincere passion for what they do that fuels their inner drive to be the best that they can be. Their mindset is sharp, focused, and unshakeable because they believe in the gifts that God had given them. They enjoy the opportunity and the challenge to compete at the highest level of the game and can never seem to get enough.

Women's Fast Pitch Softball – Best of the Best sets the stage for us to observe and recognize the accomplishments of those athletes who help shape the evolution of college softball. Thankfully, the book also identifies some of the true pioneer legends of the game and demonstrates just how much their efforts impacted future generations. Here is one example: At 15 years of age, I was put on a protected draft list for the first-ever professional league in our sport. Had I turned pro, I would have been playing for the Connecticut Falcons. However, it was at a time when female athletics was evolving. Athletic scholarships to assist attending college were just becoming available and you could not receive one if you were a professional athlete. Also, at that time, you could not represent your country in the Olympic Games if you were or had been professional. Both attending college and participating in the Olympic Games were dreams of mine so I put my pursuit of becoming a professional softball player on the back burner and looked forward to the future when I possibly could. I was very fortunate to have the opportunity to watch a couple pro league games and immediately noticed something was different; they played with a yellow ball with red seams instead of the usual all white ball, the pitching mound was at 43 feet (not 40 feet) and the outfield fences ranged from 190 feet down the lines to 220 feet in straight center field instead of equal distances all around with a minimum of 200 feet.

For many of us today, those differences do not seem so strange because they happen to be the exact same parameters seen in the college game today. The designers of that first pro league provided input into the evolving design of the college game. Many of those legends of the game are mentioned in this book. They have provided so much for the game besides dimensions and the color of the ball. They have fought the good fight and along the way have impacted others so their legacy lives on. To so many of these individuals all of us in the sport owe a huge amount of gratitude. Thank you.

So I ask you, how much do you think the pioneer legends in the game have impacted the sport today? The answer is "tremendously" and many people do not realize it. As you read this book, listen closely to the words from the more recent generation of stars and you can hear just how much those who paved the way have affected their lives. Many of these latest greats have been coached by a legend, some have been able to call a legend their teammate, others might have competed against them and even for only a game in competition or exhibition they were impacted and would never be the same. I have witnessed young athletes being introduced to one and getting an autograph and have seen the experience change their lives forever. I was one of those young girls. At the 1976 ASA Women's Major National Championships in Stratford, Connecticut, we had just finished a game and all of us on the team were seated in center field. My coach came up to me and introduced this "old-timer," as she called her, and presented me with a personalized autograph on a softball. At the time, being so young, I did not know who she was and my coach realized that and said to me, "You may not know it now, but one day you will appreciate it." The person I met that day and whose autograph I received personalized to me was the one and only Bertha Tickey. This legend in the game impacted the sport so dramatically that even today her name is on the National Championship Most Outstanding Pitcher Award. As I inquired more about her (at a time before access to the Internet), I realized that I spoke to and shook the hand of one of the greatest softball players of all time. I became instantly inspired and could not keep my eyes off that ball as I admired her and my name together on it. I felt a special something inside me and knew I, too, would commit myself to being the best I could be, as she did. I knew it was possible because this legend did it and expected from herself nothing less.

I am deeply honored to have been asked to write the foreword to *Women's Fast Pitch Softball – Best of the Best*. I have always known that God has blessed me with longevity in the sport for a reason and it is times like this that the reason becomes very clear. I have played for 30 years, starting from humble beginnings, and through it all, I remembered. From playing on a women's travel ball team at the tender age of 10 to becoming a Women's Major League team batgirl to a player and then experiencing the first NCAA College World Series, the first Pan American and Olympic Games in our sport to designing a professional softball tour, I have been very blessed to have met, seen, and competed with and against many of these Best of the Best listed. This book is to honor them and inspire us!

This book shares stories that need to be told – stories that share history but also stories that inspire and can change lives in meaningful and positive ways. But I have to admit that I find myself torn because I want more! I know there are so many more women to mention that it would be very difficult to list them all. Each one of you have made an amazing impact in our game. For all of you, too, a sincere thanks.

I love how this book connects and intertwines the past with the present. You can see how history and the people that make it affect us all. Read it and share the history of the game with us. Many of us lived it and saw it through our own eyes, but this book will help all of us bring the past more clearly into the present. Hopefully, the stories you read will inspire you to be the best that you can be in everything you do no matter how difficult or what the challenges you face might be. Every day, let's keep striving to be the *Best of the Best.*

Dot Richardson M.D.

Lisa Fernandez

Michele Smith

Natasha Watley

Cat Osterman

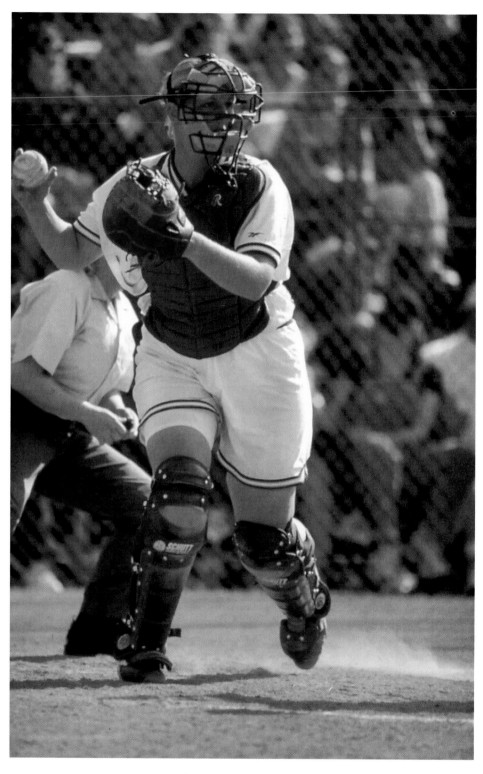

Stacey Nuveman

Jennie Finch

Monica Abbott

Dr. Dot Richardson

Shawn Andaya

Debbie Doom

Coach Mike Candrea

Joan Joyce

Coach Sue Enquist

Coach Judi Garmin ...

Carol Spanks

Coach Judi Garmin

Coach Margie Wright

Cindy Bristow

Women's *Fast Pitch* Softball

Michele Smith of the 2000 USA Olympic team proclaims the USA is No. 1 in the world after the USA beat Japan, 2-1, in the gold medal game. (Photo courtesy USA Softball)

INTRODUCTION
"BEST OF THE BEST"

Funny thing about passion: it can't be sustained without being real. And the best of the best in any field you can name have it. This is a book about women's fast pitch softball and the very few who have risen to the top of the game. We are Bill Plummer, a journalist for 50 years and Steve Clarfield, Ph.D., a practicing psychologist for 40 years. We have joined our efforts to provide a book that is as meticulous as you would expect a journalist to be and as thoughtful regarding the factors contributing to anyone's success as you would expect a psychologist to be.

We have been very fortunate because Bill personally knows everyone mentioned in this book and has received a mountain of cooperation in obtaining accurate stories told from the perspective of the participants and others who contributed to the events described.

About 50 years ago a psychologist named Abraham Maslow decided that it was important for psychology to align itself with education to investigate those factors that contribute to well-being and success. Rather than being exclusively interested in dysfunction and illness, Maslow believed that it was important for psychology to learn from excellent, healthy people in any field by getting to know them and sharing what we have learned about them. Today that field is called the Human Potential Movement because its purpose is to study state-of-the-art possibilities, or put another way, the best and most practical ways to achieve something worth obtaining.

Steve is a firm believer in the benefits of studying and collaborating with "best of the best" performers, because in addition to often-impressive physical gifts, these people have something to teach each of us on our own journey to be the best that we can be. Profiled in this book are 19 different examples of how to get where you want to be. We chose that number so there would be a sufficient variety of examples to select from to gather ideas and tips about achieving success.

Steve has worked closely with excellent performers in business as well as with people of all ages who have managed to overcome problems through psychotherapy in order to live healthy, happier lives. Steve prefers working with families, particularly families who have confused the value of Growing Smarter with having to win every contest, not only in sports but whether the child is allowed to try something her own way in school and feel the natural consequences of an incomplete plan. Neither Bill nor Steve are strangers to learning from and overcoming difficult life situations. This book, however, takes its content from the world of women's softball, and keeps the focus on these "Difference Makers" in the game we both love.

If you picked up the book because you noticed some people on the front and back covers whom you want to learn more about, enjoy the read. Bill has obtained a number of stories that were never told before, that add to the journalistic pool of information about the history of the women's game. The only surface characteristic that they all have in common is their ability to get the job done when it counted, time after time.

The two of us discussed at length some consistent traits or markers of human excellence that were part of the softball profiles which could also be found in other areas of human achievement. If you are a person who finds interesting the paths that others have taken to get from wherever they started to wherever they had to go to reach the top of the mountain, then this book will be appealing for telling a number of such stories.

Both of us share a passion for the game that grabbed each of us in our early teens. If you can resonate to that feeling yourself or know some girl who has her heart set on playing softball at the college level, then there are a number of unique features of this book that should help you. Bill has gathered a brain trust of coaches and authorities in the game that are second to none. They have been extraordinarily frank about how the new trends in recruiting are hurting players' chances of getting the kind of attention that will genuinely impress recruiters. They also have a lot to say about the role of continuous preparation and learning in helping the selected candidate get playing time at the college level. Nothing feels worse than a wasted scholarship selection and a very unhappy student athlete.

Regarding the examples in this book of modern players in today's game, the two of us consider our selected group the best of the best, and have offered a wide range of skill sets and personality types that should enable any reader to find something that the reader can use to improve what the coaches call a champion's mindset. Chapter 1 begins with the profile of Lisa Fernandez, universally recognized by coaches as having the most powerful mindset of the modern era. The succeeding chapters then move on to discuss others who found ways to overcome the challenges of their day and make positive differences in women's fast pitch softball.

Finally, if you don't have an affinity for softball or sports, remember that mythology and sports are the colloquial languages of the culture. Immigrants coming to Ellis Island who did not speak a word of English were instructed by the wise men and women in their culture to learn to play baseball. Learning about sports is a way to gain knowledge about the people who play them and have a passion for them. Many women were once denied a chance to play the game because it was thought to be too dirty and too sweaty. Today, for millions of women, the first real experience of the benefits that come with being part of something bigger than oneself through sports came through softball, partly thanks to Title IX legislation. Softball is ubiquitous in every state of the union, and top-notch Women's softball is regularly featured on national TV. A number of female employees or executives in your company may have played the game at a high school, travel or college level and may still be putting on their spikes today as weekend warriors. Understanding what all the fuss is about could build better rapport and foster improved cooperation and team building.

Bill, Steve, and Fast Pitch Softball

Bill began most of his interviews with the question "Why Softball?" which became the organizing core for the rest of the questions. The two of us thought it a fair question to answer ourselves, and surprisingly gave the same answer, "Eddie Feigner and the King and His Court." Bill's introduction occurred when he was 14 in 1958, and Steve's when Steve was 13 in 1959. Both of us attended a barnstorming tour of a four-man team that came into a town, found the biggest venue available, and played the best team in that area – their four players against your nine.

The King and His Court mostly won, but when you watched Feigner throw dead red heat between his legs, behind his back, blindfolded, on his knees, from second base and from the farthest reaches of dead center field, the final score didn't matter in the least. Bill decided that fast pitch was the game for him and migrated to it as a catcher. Steve found the highest solid wall he could throw to, (about 12 feet) drew a chalk strike zone and spent the rest of the summer trying to keep the ball from going over the wall in Chancellor Avenue playground in Newark, New Jersey and landing in Untermann Field where he saw the King do his magic.

By the time Bill was in finishing high school, he was writing high school sports stories for the local paper. That led to additional reporting work in the Air Force which led to various sportswriter positions which resulted in his obtaining a Communications Coordinator position for the Amateur Softball Association of America (ASA) in Oklahoma City, Oklahoma. He worked for the ASA in various positions for a little over thirty years. It is from that post that he met and developed relationships with all of the people whose profiles appear in the book.

Steve met Bill in 2004 when he was writing a book about men's fast pitch legend Ty Stofflet. Ty explained that he knew Bill Plummer to be the best source in the country from which to gather background information for the book. A 1973 graduate of Indiana University, Bloomington, Indiana, Bill was extremely helpful and from this a friendship was forged. Rather than try to provide all the details of

Bill's softball accomplishments, including induction into the ASA National Softball Hall of Fame, Steve quotes Bob Condron, Director of Media Services for the United States Olympic Committee (USOC). "I can't tell you how important Bill was to the USOC. He was someone who truly cared about this sport. His enthusiasm, knowledge of the sport and professionalism endeared him to the media in the United States and throughout the world. This relationship helped elevate the sport of [women's] softball to an international level of popularity and spawned an entire generation of young players who filled the spots at high schools, recreation leagues, universities and elite national teams. It also helped the U.S. to become the best team in the world."

Steve took a different path to this partnership. Being stubborn, like most softball pitchers, he worked sufficiently long and hard on his pitching motion and accuracy to get thrown out of his playground league by the next spring. (It was fair – they were playing modified and he was throwing fast pitch). However the ban was lifted every time his playground was scheduled to play another neighboring playground in some "play day" tournament.

At age fifteen, Steve asked his dad if there was someplace where he could pitch fast pitch. Budweiser, where his father worked as an electrician, happened to have a team in the north side of Newark that needed a pitcher. Twenty-five years later Steve was still playing up and down the Eastern Seaboard, mostly at Major "A" level events as well as the occasional "AA" Regional tournament. In 1977 he and Vinnie Follo's Bloomfield Town Pub team, playing from the losers' bracket, sent a team from Buffalo, NY and the Poughkeepsie Brewers home from the "AA" Regional Tournament in the same afternoon; sometimes your memory of an entire career can be reduced to a double header set of wins that go back 35 years and counting.

Steve received his B.A. from Oberlin College (3 years of varsity baseball) and his Ph.D. in clinical psychology from the University of Rochester. He maintains a clinical office and spends most of his professional time helping public, private, non-profit and for-profit organizations build competence, while improving cooperative and competitive strategies and alliances. Today this work goes under the heading of Team Building. Steve still calls it doing good by being good.

Steve's lifelong interest in women's fast pitch softball was cemented when two of his daughters decided they wanted to learn how to pitch. Julie, followed eight years later by Sarah, learned initially with Steve's help before moving over to other teachers, and both daughters eventually became captains and starting pitchers for their high school varsity softball teams. They both still play co-ed ball on occasions, and give nothing away to the guys.

Julie and later Sarah went on family trips to Pennsylvania to see college fast pitch tournaments and the Topton Invitational. There we could sit behind the plate and try to guess what the next pitch would be (location, movement and speed). The idea was that a pitcher with a variety of pitches, good control and an unpredictable sequence could beat an opponent with better movement and speed but fewer options. We also watched the WCWS, which is where many of the athletes described in these chapters made their reputations while showing grace under pressure, growing smarter, and doing good by being good.

Three Pillars of Success

As mentioned earlier, Bill collected the interviews and he and Steve compared notes about how to obtain additional information along the lines of success-building practices. Fairly early on, three themes kept reoccurring that were consistent with information Steve had regarding general patterns of success found in other pursuits. The themes are: 1) Grace Under Pressure; 2) Growing Smarter; and 3) Doing Good by Being Good. While these might sound self-explanatory at first glance, once they are defined a bit more precisely (blame the psychologist) along with specific examples (blame the journalist) the result is a bit more complex and interesting.

Grace Under Pressure

Ever since Hans Selye identified the General Adaptation Syndrome well over fifty years ago, professionals in all fields related to human behavior have been looking for ways to manage stress and optimize performance. "Grace Under Pressure" has a couple of key aspects that make an important difference in all performance activities, including softball. Optometrist Donald Teig, O.D.said, "The harder you look, the worse you see. You've got to learn to look easy." In other words peripheral vision is lost when stress levels are raised.

Cybernetics, the mathematic science of communication and control, has a Law of Requisite Variety, coined by W. Ross Ashby in *An Introduction to Cybernetics,* which says that in a closed system (like the duel between a pitcher and batter) the part of the system that is most free to vary will control the outcome. Said another way, if the pitcher has only one pitch and the batter can hit that pitch, look for a lot of line drives.

The third aspect of Grace Under Pressure was identified by coaches in this book. They call it 'mindset' which roughly translates as an ability to believe that anything that is needed will be provided for the person who wants it most. The best example of mindset, comes from Olympic Coach Mike Candrea describing Lisa Fernandez' approach to the game before it started. According to Mike, no matter what conditions existed before any game that Lisa pitched, (e.g., wind, rain, a lopsided or wrong-colored ball, sloppy field, excessive heat, etc.) those were the "just right" conditions to have a great game that day. Lisa knew that once the game started, the conditions would be the same for each team, and let the other team beat itself. This year's WCWS was consistently played in temperatures in excess of 100 degrees Fahrenheit. Two questions of mindset were asked: Who was better conditioned for the heat? Who wanted it more and could play through the discomfort?

Growing Smarter

Will Rogers explained Growing Smarter best when he said, "It's not what people know that is the problem, it's what they know that ain't so." Professionals refer to this as a problem of false confidence; you overvalue the areas where you excel while failing to actively seek out areas where you could improve. Eventually it becomes impossible for someone to learn effectively, because they believe they have nothing further to learn.

If you combine the Law of Requisite Variety with the problem of a person not knowing what he or she doesn't know, the result is a combination of ignorance and apathy, a deadly duo if winning is your goal. Competition is all about helping get the best out of your teammates while finding ways to take advantage of the weaknesses of your opponents, and by stopping learning you run the risk of your game becoming predictable. Even if you have a "lights out" single pitch, at the top levels your pitch becomes negated by the predictability that you're always going to throw it. Taking the guess work out of reacting to your opponent reduces stress, (fewer options to wonder about) and increases confidence (reducing pressure, thus improving your opponent's reaction time).

Here is where parents can help distinguish between a temporary win, which feels good for the moment, and a hard fought contest where winning takes a back seat to learning to play the game right. The saddest examples are in Little League Baseball where kids learn to throw breaking pitches that have as much devastating effect on young arms as they do opposing batters. If growing smarter were a higher value than achieving a cheap win, many more children could build their skills in the right sequence, avoid injury, and have a long and happy ball playing career.

Doing Good by Being Good

The essence of the human condition is to be able to care for something other than oneself and support something bigger than oneself. Each of the players and coaches mentioned here are testimonials to the sentiment of "giving something back to the game." Each can trace their growth and development to unselfish people who gave of themselves to provide space and support for the budding athlete or coach.

The game exists at the level of biology, psychology, social learning and philosophy. What that means is success comes when a combination of biological factors (good health habits, athletic genetics, safe preparation) are added to psychological characteristics (willingness to learn, ability to plan, developing "savvy") social learning (being a solid member of a team, playing fair, and appreciating all aspects of smart play even if performed against you) and philosophy (golden rule standards, respect for the umpires, willing to accept defeat once the final score has been put on the board.)

There is a branch of research that supports the idea that stress reduction is related to good feelings about what the person is doing as well as being in supportive surroundings. Dacher Keltner in his book *Born to be Good* makes a powerful argument that supportive social circumstances are responsible for extending people's ability to compete well. Doing Good by Being Good can be found in random acts of special sportsmanship that ask the question: "How would I have behaved, faced with the same situation?"

The example that readily comes to mind happened when a player hit a ball over the fence to win a game, but she broke her leg swinging at the pitch. If members of her team picked her up or helped her in any way, she would have been out. The umpires were specifically forbidden to help either team in any way. So we could have had a player who hit the ball out of the park, either crawl on her belly to make it around the bases, doing whatever further damage to a broken leg or had her be rushed to a hospital while her team absorbed the loss. Instead, the captains from the other team picked her up carefully, and walked her to each base where she could touch each base and get credit for her home run fairly struck.

The Book's Structure

As you probably have gathered by now, there are separate and shared areas of expertise that came into play in the writing of this book. Bill is solely responsible for the selection of the primary nineteen All-Stars, plus an additional 56 listed in brief in the last chapter of the book. Neither of us expect complete agreement from anyone else on the selected 19, but if you can't find your candidate in a specific chapter or in the encapsulated descriptions in Chapter 20, contact Bill.

Also, anytime the word "I" appears in the chapters it will be from Bill's first-person perspective because it will describe something Bill directly saw or participated in. From time to time there will be descriptions about softball situations that could come from Bill and/or Steve. Between the two of us there is a combined 100 years of admiration for the game. The descriptions are meant for those who do not possess a deep familiarity with the women's game. Remember, part of our intent is to attract people to this outstanding game. If, for example, you already know what it means to have Natasha Watley on first base in a close game, bear with us as the build-up of drama is explained to others.

When we move to more personality-based descriptions of why people do what they do and what separates the best of the best from the others, the focus shifts to Steve's experience and expertise. The organization of material within the three pillars is also within Steve's domain.

Hopefully we will have interwoven the different aspects so seamlessly that you won't recognize where the second baseman's territory stops and the shortstop's begins. What matters most is that these are terrific people to get to know better and we hope you have some fun while doing so.

We are at a time in the history of women's fast pitch softball when it is possible to see well played games as close as your local high school, college or travel league. Unlike baseball, the games don't stretch over two and a half hours, and 60 feet of distance between bases means that play is up close and very personal. Take the opportunity to see the next generation of players who will become featured in the years to come. It is always nice to be able to say that you watched the next Monica Abbott play when she was 10, before she was cemented as the next Monica Abbott. There was something special about the way she leaned forward, looked down and let it rip, even then.

Part 1

Modern Era Athletes

Lisa Fernandez not only led the NCAA in batting her senior year, 1993, with a .510 batting average but in earned run average as well (0.25). She is the only player in NCAA history to have accomplished this feat. (Photo courtesy UCLA Sports Information)

Chapter 1

LISA FERNANDEZ
"THE COMPLETE PACKAGE"

Grace Under Pressure

S ince her debut at UCLA in 1990, after being the high school player of the year in California, Lisa Fernandez has been the most admired, respected and feared competitor in the last twenty years of women's fast pitch softball. Accolades can be directly traced to Sharron Backus and Sue Enquist, her coaches at UCLA, and Ralph Raymond and Mike Candrea, Olympic coaches during 1996-2000 and 2004, respectively. These coaches collectively describe Lisa as being in a class by herself because of her outstanding individual achievements and longevity at the top echelon of the sport.

Coach Backus, who coached Lisa and played against the other top-mentioned softball phenom Joan Joyce (see Chapter 13), sees the two pitcher/hitters as the best of their eras with Lisa possessing the kind of constant intensity that intimidates as it dominates, while Joyce more calmly made it clear that if she was having a good day, there was simply nothing that the other team was going to be able to do about it no matter how long the game lasted.

Coach Enquist traces Lisa's indomitable will to experiences

Career Highlights
(Pitcher and Third Base)

- *Led UCLA to two NCAA titles, 1990 and 1992*
- *Led UCLA to two second place WCWS 1991 and 1993 WCWS All-Tournament 1990, 1991 and 1992*
- *In 1993 Gold Medalist in Intercontinental Cup in Holland 1991, 1992, and 1993 named Honda Award Winner as college softball's best player*
- *In 1993 named Best Women's College Athlete –All Sports*
- *Finished college career with 0.22 ERA (2nd best all-time)*
- *Compiled 93-7 record with 74 shutouts in college career*
- *Finished college career- .930 winning percentage (2nd best all time)*
- *Batted .410 junior year and .510 senior year.*
- *Compiled .382 batting college batting average with 15 homers and 128 RBIs*
- *NCAA Top VI Award, presented to the top six student athletes in all divisions.*
- *1990, 1994, and 1998 Gold Medalist at ISF World Championship*
- *1996, 2000, and 2004 Olympic Gold Medalist.*
- *1992 Gold Medalist in Women's World Challenge Cup, Beijing*
- *1994 Gold Medalist South Pacific Classic in Sydney, Australia*
- *1999 Gold Medalist in Canada Cup in Surrey, British Columbia*
- *Led USA team to a 10-0 record during the 1997 Challenge Series against China and Australia. She was 3-0 with a 0.32 ERA and 43 strikeouts.*

she had with other UCLA influences, particularly Dot Richard-son, NCAA player of the 1980's decade. Dot made it acceptable to pursue full-out commitment to achieving top tier goals like national and international championships and to accept responsibility when less than full effort contributed to losses to inferior teams. Coach Enquist points out a little-known fact, which can be verified in the opening picture: that Lisa has very small hands for a pitcher and had to work additionally hard to get the ball and bat to behave according to her will.

Being 5 feet 6 inches also contributed to Lisa's extraordinary work habits, forcing her to get to the gym wherever she was and whenever she could. Coach Raymond noted that it was not unusual to find Lisa on her way to the gym at 10 p.m. after a full day's work-out. Coach Raymond is a stickler for keeping the game simple and executing well. He believed that giving a game away to the opposition because of insufficient physical or mental preparation was something that should bother the person who gave less than her full measure. In his estimation, Lisa was right up there with Dot as the two hardest workers who had ever played for him.

Mike Candrea considered Lisa remarkable in a few other ways. He was most impressed with her ability to be unpredictable while, in his words, "reinventing herself" to stay at the top of the talent curve. The fact that she did this continuously for twenty years is, he believes, a testament to her creativity and ingenuity. She is the most cited master of requisite variety in the book.

Coach Candrea also described Lisa's mindset as her most powerful asset. According to Candrea, "Lisa was smart enough to know that there was an emotional phase of the game that you had to learn how to control, but you can't control it unless you put yourself in that environment as often as possible. She would play little games with herself on (international) tours, even when the score was 10-0, or when she was throwing in the bullpen.

She was readying herself for the next gold medal game. How many athletes really understand that? They wonder why. You always see it. The kid who hits the cover off the ball during batting practice every day, but gets in a game where all of a sudden she is amped up. As a result, these kids can't control their body parts and can't perform."

Lisa agrees. "I try to set up situations where what I do in practice feels like what I do in games. There is no difference in pressure because all my pitches, whether thrown in the bullpen or in a tight game, feel like the real thing." Lisa also had fun learning new things about the game every day she could. "I would take information that anybody could give me and could figure out how to apply it until the end of my career. I always wanted to learn how I could do things better and more efficiently."

Growing Smarter

Ask Lisa Fernandez which particular softball skill she performed better than anyone else and she will be quick to point out that her best skill was learning new skills. She is not being coy or modest; that isn't Lisa's style. Fernandez became one of the best who ever played the game by daring to make honest appraisals of her skills and continuously finding ways to get better by growing smarter. Perhaps it is the kind of thinking that comes with graduating as a psychology major and being honored as a Top VI Award Student Athlete. Or it just might go along with her mother and father's belief that constant self-imposed challenges are the key to avoiding fear of losing. In Lisa's family, hollow victories – games played against relatively weak competition – were to be avoided at all cost. It was much better to play against an older, bigger group of girls and get beat than to coast to meaningless victories.

If you were to change the subject and ask her who she knew who worked more diligently than she did to grow and develop her skills, she would be hard pressed to describe anyone. It is not difficult to find a few who are mentioned along with her, but doing more than she did might just turn out to be impossible. It is part of softball lore that Lisa's preparation program lasted nearly every day of every year she played at the top level of the game.

Lisa's goal has always been to improve at every facet of the game. She can describe days indoors when she was eleven, diving for balls just out of her reach as preparation for making that play at third base. Although she did not get a chance to play any position other than pitcher in high school, once she got to UCLA she was able to play a little more than half of her games at third base.

Her approach to hitting and pitching is based on the idea that players who can cover the entire strike zone will give their opponents much more to think about than those who favor a part of it. As a pitcher Lisa developed six different pitches she could use in a game, including a rise ball, drop, and changeup that could be thrown anywhere in the count. She also describes with matter-of-fact candor that it was her goal to be a hitter who could cover the inside of the plate with an expected .500 batting average, while being able to cover the outside of the plate also at a .500 average. She expected to cover all speeds of pitched balls at a .500 average. "I wanted to have the best eye in the country."

Part of the legend of Lisa Fernandez rests on a few events very early in her softball life. At age 8, after having only pitched to her mom in the backyard, she had her first experience against another team with an umpire. "I lost 28 – 0 and walked batters with the bases loaded, hit batters. I think I walked more than 20." She also threw as though she were in a slow pitch game (her parents played together on a slow pitch team). Lisa remembers her parents' reaction. They suggested that she could use that first game to gauge her improvement in future games. And that is how she went about judging her abilities on the softball field.

The famed Lisa Fernandez work ethic came out of those early years and was only helped by comments made by insensitive adults who decided that it was their duty to dissuade Lisa from playing ball. The pattern of criticism will become familiar throughout the book. Why do you want to be a strong girl? Why aren't you spending more time actively preparing to become somebody's wife? There is just something wrong about watching women in strenuous exercise – what's wrong with you for wanting to do that? In Lisa's case, her primary buffer from this nonsense was her father, who immediately understood his daughter's build (she describes herself as stocky and strong even as a young child) and encouraged her to make the most of her God-given abilities.

No matter who attempted to be negative about her aspirations, Lisa's parents made it clear that the most important thing to them was the effort that she put into the games she played, not whether she won or lost. As long as she was trying her best and making improvement, she could always count on their support.

There is also a story about a children's team coach who concluded that one of the most highly motivated and potentially coachable young girls ever to put on a uniform was in that talent evaluator's opinion not a suitable candidate for the league she was trying to join. Of course, some stories are so outrageous that they just make you shake your head and wonder.

Since her family was not wealthy, there wasn't a budget set aside for special teachers to show her the finer points of the game. It is, however, hard to imagine a world with women's softball that doesn't include the exploits of Lisa Fernandez, and at age 11, Lisa caught a break. From ages 11 to 18, she played for Larry Mays, coach of the Gordon's Panthers, a team sponsored by Gordon Mullins. According to Lisa, Larry Mays entered her life at a critical time. "I couldn't have learned more about the game from anybody else." Gordon's Panthers won 6 ASA age group National Championships and Lisa credits them with providing sufficient grounding in softball to be prepared for her college years at UCLA with Coach Backus.

"Doing Good by Being Good"

In 1990, Lisa joined the UCLA Bruins, NCAA Softball's first dynasty. At the beginning of the season, Sharron Backus made it clear that it was her intention to win another Women's College World Series for their school. Players were expected to make a full commitment to that goal, and anything less would be unacceptable. Since Lisa's list of high school accomplishments included a career ERA of 0.07 for Lakewood St. Joseph (second best all-time) including 37 no-hitters and 12 perfect games, she would be counted on heavily right from the start of her college career.

The Bruins were a family where the more experienced players served as mentors for their younger, inexperienced teammates. According to Lisa, "It was Dot who said, 'It's okay to love this game. There's nothing wrong with that.' I've just been blessed to have people in my life who have been able to support what I loved to do and allowed me to believe it was okay."

Contact with Coach Backus and players of her generation made Lisa feel fortunate that she had her most productive years when National and International competitions were flourishing. We will be focusing first on Lisa's college years, which occurred simultaneously with her tenure on the USA National Team, beginning in 1990 and running continuously for over a decade. Suffice it to say that wherever Lisa played she had a substantial impact on the game.

UCLA in 1990 was coming off two consecutive World Series Championships. Being surrounded by a team loaded with talent throughout the lineup provided a fun way to begin her college career, as UCLA also won the WCWS that year. Lisa was voted to the first of four All-American teams, one for each of her college campaigns.

In 1991, UCLA was favored to win their fourth consecutive championship during her sophomore year, but something was definitely missing. She believes that the team took winning a bit for granted and might have underestimated their University of Arizona opponents. The result was a 5-1 loss in the championship game, accompanied by a very bad sense that the less-talented team had prepared better and wanted to win more than the perennial champs. Lisa said she felt she had let down her family, her team and her school by not putting out everything she had. The individual honors kept accumulating, but she is definitely one of those athletes who could care less about an individual prize when the team goal has been taken away.

For a number of athletes cited in this book, caring about the welfare of the team and enjoying the pleasure of their company is the top reason for playing the game. Lisa Fernandez was rapidly becoming one of the best players in the modern game, yet was thoroughly caught up in the championship that got away. She didn't claim some sort of foul play or bothered to blame a teammate. Her focus was about what would have to happen in 1992 to make the bad feelings go away and all answers led to higher levels of dedication while pushing herself to an unprecedented level of excellence.

These are the 1992 statistics compiled by Lisa Fernandez. She won 29 straight games, including pitching 26 scoreless innings in the WCWS – for those of you who enjoy unsurpassable lifetime statistics, that means she had a 0.00 ERA in the WCWS. In the five WCWS games, UCLA won by a combined score of 31 – 1. I guess the moral of this story is this: "Don't get Lisa Fernandez looking for revenge on a softball field."

Lisa's senior year, 1993, included a feat that no other ballplayer, with the exception of baseball's Babe Ruth, had the combined skill sets to manage. She batted .510 (yes, five ten) for the entire season, which to this day remains in the record book, while compiling a season ERA of 0.25, which led all Division One players. She wound up losing 1-0, again to the Arizona Wildcats in the WCWS, but this time there was no talk of Lisa doing less than her full share to help her team win.

Fernandez was a double threat, from the mound as well as at-bat, compiling a .382 career batting average at UCLA. (Photo courtesy UCLA Sports Information Department)

Michele Smith compiled an 82-20 pitching record and batted .343
during her college career at Oklahoma State University.
(Photo courtesy Oklahoma State Archives.)

Chapter 2

MICHELE SMITH
"TENACITY AND PERSEVERANCE"

Grace Under Pressure

The picture on the left was provided by Oklahoma State University where Michele Smith spent her college years. She looks every bit the athlete: 5 feet 10 inches, well-proportioned, and steely-eyed. Pitchers do not go into a pitching-ready position with a smile on their face. It's considered bad sportsmanship. It's okay to strike the batter out but a smile suggests lack of respect. So even in this publicity photo, game propriety is something you can count on Michele to observe.

The reason that this photo was selected for the beginning of this chapter is that this is about the age when Michele's ordered life as an athlete was threatened with extinction. Athletes are taught when they are young to distinguish between soreness and injury, but when a freakish accidental injury occurs which tears away parts of a pitcher's throwing arm, this represents a much higher level of crisis. Usual concerns after an injury include "How

13

Career Highlights
(Pitcher, First Base)

• *Member of USA National Team 1991-2002*
• *Two-time Olympic Gold Medalist, 1996 and 2000 for USA team*
• *Two-time Pan Am Gold Medalist, 1995 and 1999, for USA team*
• *Two-time winner (1993-94) of USOC Softball Woman of the year*
• *Two-time ASA Softball Sportswoman of the Year, 1990 and 1994*
• *Three-time ASA National Tournament MVP*
• *ISF World Championship Gold Medalist, 1994,1998, 2002*
• *Four-time Bertha Tickey Award winner 1990, 1993-95 as outstanding pitcher*
• *Named ASA All-American 10 times, leading team to 3 ASA national titles, 1993-95 and two runners-up, 1992 and 1998*
• *Compiled 82-20 pitching record at OSU (0.74 ERA in 707 innings)*
• *Compiled .343 career batting average at OSU*
• *Won eight Japan Softball League MVP awards out of 15 possible*
• *Won eight Japan Softball League titles out of 15 possible*
• *1988-89 NCAA All-American, All Academic Big Eight Conference, All Region, Honda Award runner-up, Dean's list*
• *Inducted into ASA National Hall of Fame (2006), Oklahoma Sports Hall of Fame (2010), New Jersey ASA Hall of Fame (2008), Shasta County Sports Hall of Fame, (1998), NJSIAA/Bollinger High School Hall of Fame (1998)*
• *1990 graduate of Oklahoma State in health wellness and pre-med*

much rest do I need to have before I can go back to my team?" Here the usual concerns are replaced by questions such as "Am I facing a career ending injury?"

Michele recounted the details of her injury in her book, *Michele Smith's Book of Good Softball Cheer* in the chapter on Perseverance (p.38). On July 21, 1986, the summer after her freshman year at Oklahoma State University, driving home with her father from an oral surgeon's appointment, her passenger side door flew open as her dad was turning a corner. She was thrown from the truck into a roadside post, chopping off part of her elbow bone and tearing the triceps and nerve endings in her left (pitching) arm.

Go back to the picture and look at the epitome of an athlete. For this sort of injury to such a delicate part of the throwing arm, however, no doctor would think of pronouncing the injury temporary. In fact, it is their task to let the athlete know that life after freak accidents does not always revert to a smooth continuation of life before the accident. Some parts of their lives may not continue at all. That is why this story belongs within Grace Under Pressure: because Michele Smith faced the specter of life without athletics and made two decisions. She would certainly continue living as a good person no matter what, but first she and those who believed in her rehabilitation would have something to say about the path her future would take.

If you look at the Oklahoma State University website, which honors Michele's induction into the school's Sports Hall of Fame, you can hear the pride in the voices of the coaches who were aware of the gargantuan effort she and her trainers performed, first to help her regain strength and range of motion and later to rebuild her pitching motion. To say that this is a physically painful process is a fair understatement. In the absence of happy ending guarantees it is also a measure of strong personal faith, tenacity and perseverance.

Prior to her rehabilitation, Michele Smith could throw fast. After her rehab she was three miles faster. Whatever she did to get those three miles per hour into her delivery, rest assured that she worked for every bit of it. In addition, Michele can say that she faced down the demons of athletic destruction and made them turn and run. After that it is our guess that nothing on the ball field would be as intimidating for the rest of her career. Based on what she had to do to stay in the game it is no surprise that she has had very important roles in the game to this day, eight years after she retired in 2003.

Growing Smarter

Michele Smith played softball from the time she was 5, but unlike the other pitchers mentioned in this book, she didn't go to the mound until she was a sophomore at Voorhees High School in Califon, New Jersey. Smith starred in three sports for her school, basketball, field hockey and softball, and expressed an interest in basketball. "I loved basketball. It was challenging but I got three times as many softball scholarships. I advanced quickly in softball so it made sense to go in that direction."

There is an advantage to taking up a special skill like pitching in your teens, especially if you are a quick study and can find an excellent teacher. Michele had a number of good coaches who over the years taught her the finer points of the game, but when discussing pitching she gives credit to Betty Zwingraf, who provided a solid foundation which she used for the rest of her career.

When Michele was 17 she entered Major ASA team competition. She credits her parents, Ernest and Barbara, for helping her make that jump. "They taught me discipline. Things weren't going to be easy. There is no cakewalk. It was either sink or swim, but I learned not to be afraid and embrace the challenge as an opportunity."

At each new level, even before her accident, Michele had a knack for finding opportunities to learn and grow smarter. "College was a great experience for me. I came from a small high school and it was terrific getting to meet new people from other states."

Once the accident occurred, Michele had to become even more resourceful. First she had to rethink who she was at her core: Was she an athlete or a person? She came to the conclusion that the person is more important than any particular set of abilities she possesses. "The doctors told me that I might never pitch again. It was like losing my identity." So she dug deep and found the fortitude to get through the pain and uncertainty to find out what was on the other side. In her situation, the love of the game and her investment in getting back into it returned her to a higher level than she had ever experienced before.

I met Michele at a reception when she was a sophomore at OSU. She was friendly, easy to talk to, smart, and articulate. Even then, she had all the features that we have learned to expect from her as an announcer and commentator for ESPN during women's college fast pitch softball games as well as other events she has been assigned to cover. During my years at the ASA, when she was in town, she would make it a point to stop by and say hello. I was able to watch her play over thirty games because she was an Oklahoma neighbor when she wasn't an international traveler.

Michele's career statistics are unprecedented in my experience as a sports journalist. There are many athletes who worked hard after an accident to regain former skills. For example, Tommy John surgery helps pitchers get close to how they used to throw. I can't cite another example where somebody had a terrible accident, did an extensive rehab that took a full nine months and wound up throwing harder than before. Michele will also tell any person who asks that she was able to do this while throwing five different pitches with tournament-ready accuracy and effectiveness. I don't believe she is bragging. Given her forthright personality she is certainly being accurate about just what is possible when an excellent set of trainers and a disciplined and determined athlete put their combined minds to the problem.

During her four years at OSU, Smith earned All-America honors twice (her junior and senior years), compiled an 82-20 record overall and batted .393 and .379 in her junior and senior years. She was a three-time All-Big Eight selection, two-time All-Big Eight Academic selection. Her junior and senior batting averages were over 100 points better than her freshman and sophomore stats.

After college she went on to ASA and USA Softball where she continued to improve every facet of her game. There is also a bit of the gunslinger mentality in her play. When I asked her about a game that stood out in her mind after college ball, she quickly went to the 1993 ASA National Championship in Stratford, Conn. Listen carefully to the next story and you'll hear the theme of how an unwelcome group of strangers came into town to do their jobs against all odds.

"We (the Redding Rebels) beat the Brakettes two games in a row to win the national championship. No one had ever really done that before, winning two games in a row on their field with 5,000 fans cheering against us. I think we had five fans for us. That was a pretty big victory and I think it was good for the game." Smith came on in relief in the first game and pitched the second game.

The following year the Redding Rebels were also the ASA National Champions. Michele went 5-0 with a 0.00 ERA and 47 strikeouts in 33 innings to win the Bertha Tickey Award as the country's outstanding pitcher. This time the Rebels had to go 9-1 with eight games in the loser's bracket. As has certainly been made clear, the more difficult the prize, the more interested Michele Smith is in attaining it.

During 1994-96, Smith's attention shifted to the international game with China as the USA's top opponent. "In this period, China was so good that the games were always epic every time Team USA and China stepped on the field together. It was going to be extra innings, each game kinda came down to the wire."

By 1996 Michele was a mainstay of the USA Olympic Team, coached by Ralph Raymond, whose Brakettes Michele had faced and defeated in Stratford. In the Pre-Olympic Tour, Michele went 12-0 with a 0.00 ERA and batted .326. In Atlanta, Georgia, Smith went 2-0 with a 1.50 ERA and 23 strikeouts in 14 innings. In 2000 at the Sydney Australia Olympic Games she finished the tournament with a 0.00 ERA and 37 strikeouts in 27.2 innings. Michele threw a 14-inning two-hitter against China, but a defensive error allowed two unearned runs to score to end the game. Errors also cost Smith against Japan, when she threw 5.2 innings of relief before three errors in the top of the 11th cost the USA two unearned runs. Michele pitched eight shutout innings against China in the first playoff game before being relieved.

Doing Good by Being Good

Even as a sophomore at OSU there was something mature and effectively caring about the way Michele engaged in relationships with everyone she encountered on and off the field. Countless times, I have seen her go out of her way to accommodate fan requests, both as a player and TV personality. Her interest in the game has extended to being a member of the committee that is working to bring the game back into the Olympics. I can't think of anyone I'd rather have as an articulate spokesperson to represent the game.

Michele and her way of playing the game have been mentioned by at least two of our best of the best, Jennie Finch and Cat Osterman, who mentioned her as a role model for how they approach being a softball champion and celebrity. Michele, for her part, was generous in reaching out and keeping track with players and their families. That sort of special attention is appreciated because it can't be faked.

There is another part of her career that is unique and fits under Doing Good by Being Good. It concerns Michele's sixteen years (1993-2008) as a venerated star in the Japanese Professional Softball league. "I won over 100 games in Japan. I know it doesn't sound like a lot but the first couple of years there we played only twelve to fourteen games a year. When it comes to high quality games I think my record is between 150 and 160 wins." She added, "I was named MVP eight times out of fifteen championships I played in. In the fifteen championships, we won eight and we never finished lower than third."

As Michele looks back on her career she can't help but feel a sense of accomplishment. "I was really blessed," said Smith, "I think the biggest thing was that I was able to stay at the top of my game for as long as I did. And that actually had to do with my training. I was very passionate about my practice. If there is one thing I am really proud of it's the fact that the last year of my career I was still throwing the ball close to 70 miles an hour, and I was one of the best batters on our team. What I was most proud of was that people were surprised that I retired while I was playing so well. They thought I should have played for another year or two at least. For me, it was really time to move on and to challenge myself in another area."

As Michele Smith represents the interests of international softball to the Olympic Committee, or teaches one of her many clinics, or even spends time with fans from all over the world, I for one am very pleased that my friend made the most of her opportunity to beat back adversity and reclaim her athletic identity. To this day she calls the accident one of the best things that happened to her, because it made the young girl at the beginning of this chapter face what she really wanted and appreciate what she would have to do to turn her hopes and aspirations into a best of the best career.

(From left) Jessica Mendoza, Michele Smith and Beth Mowins comprise the ESPN broadcasting team for the NCAA Women's College World Series in Oklahoma City. (ESPN Photo)

Natasha Watley earned All-American honors four times during her career at UCLA. (Photo courtesy of UCLA Sports Information)

Chapter 3

NATASHA WATLEY
"SPEED AND INSPIRATION"

Grace Under Pressure

Natasha Watley believes that her college years were pivotal in helping her grow as an athlete and a person. "When playing with other elite athletes, it felt rewarding to know that we all had a commonality in striving for excellence and winning. Yes, there was a lot of pressure to be the best. It is easy to say that you want to be the best but having to live that, day in and day out, can become stressful. I eventually learned to turn pressure into motivation. Working hard and staying positive can ease pressure. It's only pressure when you let it become pressure. Whenever softball became a grind for me, I always reminded myself that it was a choice to play, not something demanded of me."

Softball is a sport that cherishes its winners, but every winner has to be able to manage defeat and defeat feels like dropping into a hole. Nobody wins every game in their career. Here's Natasha's perspective on how to deal with the inevitable losses and climb out of holes that they create: "Softball has taught me about managing failure by thinking about failure as minor setbacks or even as motivations. I always seem to find some positives

Career Highlights
(Shortstop)

- Twice member of the USA Olympic Team, 2004 and 2008
- First African American to play softball in Olympics
- Winner of the Honda Broderick Award and Pac 10 Player of the Year senior year 2003
- Four-time All-American at UCLA, led team to three WCWS
- Led UCLA to national title in 2003
- Twice was leading hitter in WCWS, 2002 (.462) and 2003 (.440)
- In four years at UCLA compiled a .450 batting average with 395 hits, 252 runs scored and 158 stolen bases.
- In 2002, had a 32-game hit streak, fifth longest in NCAA history
- First UCLA player to have 100 plus hit seasons, 2002 and 2003
- Twice named to WCWS All-Tournament team 2002 and 2003
- Twice a finalist for USA Softball Player of the Year, 2002, 2003
- Two-time gold medalist in Pan Am Games 2003 (.292); 2007 (.364)
- Two-time gold medalist in ISF World Championship, 2002, 2006
- In 2002, named All-Tourney Canada Cup and MVP in ISF World Championship
- Three-time member of World Cup Championship team, 2006, 07, 09
- Named first team ASA All-American in 2000 for Team Texas
- In 2010 batted .402, stole 14 bases to lead USSSA Pride to NPF Championship. Named MVP of National Pro Fastpitch Series
- Currently a member of Team Toyota in the Japan Softball League.

in all my setbacks because there is always a greater perspective than what I'm experiencing at that exact moment." Lisa Fernandez is a key figure for helping her deal with the ups and downs of the game. "Lisa has taught me that hard work truly pays off and never to stop learning about the game, no matter what age you are in your career." As for Sue Enquist, "She effectively manipulated my mindset to make me believe that I could walk on water if I put my mind to it. I could always reinvent myself but it starts with my own mindset."

UCLA was also the place where Natasha found outlets for her off-the-field aspirations. Look at a listing of Natasha Watley's accomplishments and you will see "First African-American on the USA Olympic Team." She doesn't make too much of this designation, but she doesn't make too little of it either. Watley reports being acutely aware of the absence of black female on-the-field role models and having made a conscious choice to be a one-person difference maker for the next generation.

Spend some time around Natasha and you can feel the intensity that sits just under her quiet reserve. She is never going to bore you with statements regarding what she is about to do. That feels too much like bragging. The best way to understand Natasha Watley is to see what she and those around her can accomplish and get a sense of the respect others have for her dedication to her ideals and her ability to get things done and done well.

Difference makers quickly detect the importance of bringing something special to the pursuit of their goals and getting the best out of the people who help them. If you played ball during a period when you couldn't find positive role models who looked like you and you wanted to change that situation for the next generation, what college subjects would you want to study? When you look at Natasha's resume you will find a sociology degree with a minor in African studies. Here is where preparation goes beyond the ball field and into the classroom. Later, when it is time to turn the plan into positive deeds, she finds that she has also turned herself into a multiple-tool player here as well.

Growing Smarter

Imagine a 14-under team that had Jennie Finch as their pitcher and Natasha Watley as their shortstop. Where do you think they finished in the ASA 14-and-under Nationals? In the picture that opens the Finch chapter, that same duo appears in their USA Olympic team uniforms about 10 years later congratulating each other. When Jennie Finch is mentioned as the face of USA softball, that is the face I tend to see: determined, focused, and connected to a teammate. As for Natasha Watley, she is supporting and acknowledging what is happening on the field from her position right in the center of the action.

If you played against Natasha, the picture on the left could cause nightmares and loss of sleep. She has put the bat on the ball – if it bounces more than twice, don't even bother making the throw to first. Nothing good can happen (she's already past the bag), but a number of bad outcomes are likely. Once she is on, you know that one of the most dangerous base stealers of all-time is poised at first base, and heading out to second on her own, stealing the base. She can take advantage of the extra bit of nervousness that occurs when a pitcher and catcher have to change their plan because off-speed pitches can't outrun dazzling foot speed.

It is easy to look into the record book and find the 158 stolen bases that she is credited for during her four-time All-American career at UCLA. What is not available in the scorebook are all those times when respect for and concern about her speed caused something to happen that worked in UCLA's favor. It might have been a pitch that went flat because the pitcher was trying to get the ball to the plate too quickly, or an extra bit of urgency on the catcher's part to be in a ready throwing position that caused the ball to glance off her mitt, or a wild pitch resulting from lack of full attention to the pitch. When Natasha is on first base there are plenty of good reasons to expect her to be on second without putting an out into the scorebook.

Put Natasha on second and home plate is her next thought. She knows it, and all the fielders know it as well. A grounder to second base might be bobbled or thrown in haste because Natasha is behind the fielder and no one knows where she might be on the base paths. Put a ball in the outfield and we're now the other team must make sure that somebody else doesn't move up a base. Natasha is already back on the bench enjoying the high fives and encouraging more of this merriment for her team.

Nobody starts out as a college standout. Years of being a player and teammate set the background for later stardom. When you ask Natasha Watley, "Why softball?"you quickly pick up her learning strategies. "You can try and master so many different skills. The game doesn't discriminate by shape or size. You can be tall and successful and short and successful. You can possibly only be a great hitter, a great pitcher, or even a great fielder and still contribute to your team or you can be all of the above. I honestly just thoroughly loved playing the game and being around my teammates. I'm an only child so being with my team was like having built-in best friends or sisters. I don't remember a specific moment that made me realize that I was dedicating my life to softball. That's the way it worked out."

Sue Enquist, her coach at UCLA, told me that she was the most enjoyable player she ever coached. Coaches of dynasties tend to be much more careful about making that sort of blanket statement, so when I asked why, here is what she said: "First, she had so much respect for the uniform, for the university, for her teammates and her coaches. She had humility about how good she was and despite being in an environment where I was constantly pushing her, I felt like she was willing to take the risk to be more versatile. She came in as a slapper and a short-gamer and I was really interested in opening up her game, having her be a double threat at the plate. I think that was a really big step for her and she went for it. Tasha became one of our leading RBI and home run hitters when she was a Bruin. A lot of people don't know that. It was a lot of fun watching her game continue to expand and grow and eventually become an Olympian, one of our sport's greatest ever. And to win the Honda Broderick Cup as the best female college athlete put her right up there with Lisa Fernandez, softball's only other recipient.

"And through all of it, Natasha never changed. She had zero ego unless she was in the batter's box. It made coaching her extremely fun." There are other comments from Coach Enquist about her most enjoyable player but they will wait for another section. Stacey Nuveman, who was a teammate on both the Bruins and the Olympic team, identified Watley as "the most unpretentious superstar you will ever meet. She is very humble, very giving, laughs easily and loves being in the company of her teammates. There were many times I recall her laughing so hard she would cry, whether it was laughing at herself or something someone said or a situation. She was never the most vocal leader, but led by example. She never slacked in practice, even if she made things look easy. I never coached her, but she was always open to coaching and very respectful to the coaching staff."

Enquist's comments are supported by the record. During Natasha's freshman year she hit one homer, ten doubles and four triples. In her sophomore year she hit two homers, nine doubles and five triples followed by her junior year where she hit two homers, 14 doubles and 7 triples. By her senior year, her ten homers was third best on the team. She also hit 12 doubles and 5 triples. The most compelling statistic is found in her season RBI totals. In her four college seasons, beginning as a freshman, her RBI totals increased from 11 in her freshman year to 36 as a sophomore, 35 as a junior, and finally 53 during her senior year.

As a junior and senior at Woodbridge High School, she was named second team All-American. She hit over .445 in her last three seasons and stole more than 20 bases per season. The result was a tryout for the USA team before she went to UCLA.

Coachability is about being able to detect what changes can be accomplished to get to an unprecedented level of performance and devote fully concentrated effort toward doing that. Natasha is bright and resourceful. When Sue Enquist describes the partnership that molded Natasha into a five tools player (run, throw, field, hit, hit with power) it was Natasha's extreme coachability that set her apart and allowed her to gain those skills that give her opponents even more to worry about.

At the conclusion of her four-year college career, she was in the top ten in career batting average, (.450) top three for career hits (395), top five in career runs (252) and top ten in career stolen bases (158). After leading her team to the 2003 WCWS and garnering the top honors that women's college sports has to offer, Natasha continued to make her mark for Team USA.

She began playing for Team USA in 2001, and it is not surprising that she was named Most Inspirational Player at the Canada Cup. In 2004 she batted .400 in the Olympics with nine hits and ten RBI. She was a three-time member of the World Cup Championship team in 2006, 2007 and 2009. In 2008, when the USA Olympic team won the silver medal, Watley batted .321 with six RBI and two home runs.

Natasha Watley began her professional international career in 2007 in Japan where she plays for Team Toyota in the Japan Softball League. She also plays in the NPF where in 2010 she batted .402, and stole 14 bases to lead the USSSA Pride to the National Professional Fastpitch Championship. Watley was named MVP of the Championship Series.

Doing Good by Being Good

We go back to Coach Enquist's perspective about Natasha Watley: "I think she cared so much about her teammates, she would be the type of person that would stay after practice and hit fungous to the outfielders or hit fungous to her roommate, Monique Mejia. She is someone who is extremely interested in helping the inner city and being a messenger [of the idea] that no matter what color you are, the game doesn't know how much money is in your pocket. She partnered with the Major League Baseball RBI program and became such a fixture in the City of Los Angeles that the City of Los Angeles Park and Recreation has named a league after Natasha Watley. I don't know of any other player that has that honor. I think it says an awful lot about her integrity. I couldn't be more proud of her. You meet her parents and you can see why. They instilled in her respect, class, and grace and she has carried it out to this day. She's only a phone call away. Whenever you need anything, Natasha will be there for you and that's just great."

The Natasha Watley Foundation has as its mission "to empower young women to make healthy lifestyle choices, develop strong self-esteem and to become leaders of character through participation and training in the sport of softball." The official website includes four core foundation goals. "1) Confidence development: by use of positive role models and affiliations that will contribute to all facets of life, especially when participation with the NWF is over. 2) Women's Health: increasing a positive body image as both a female and an athlete. 3) Social Issues: decreasing matters adversely affecting underserved communities such as teen pregnancy, gang affiliations, and high school drop out rates. And 4) 4 Points of the Diamond: as based on the core values of the NWF; discipline, dedication, dignity and duty." With regard to programs, "NWF participants will be receiving technical instruction from the world's most elite softball athletes. The Four Points are instilled in the girls through mentoring, role modeling, and a structured curriculum that will transcend the softball diamond." The website then goes on to describe 12-under and high school club leagues which have included over 200 participants and mention ways that individuals and groups can partner with the Foundation.

This summer Team Watley went to the 10-under Class A Fast Pitch ASA National Championships in Johnson City, Tennessee. The team was coached by Robert Young and included 12 players. Thirty-one teams participated in the tournament. Team Watley went 5-0 to win the championship. The team's pitchers didn't allow a run – all shutouts: 12-0, 1-0, 17-0, 4-0 and 7-0.

Team Watley after the team won the Class A ASA 10-and-under National Championship in 2011 (photo courtesy of Mike Carmo)

Former University of Texas pitcher Cat Osterman compiled a 59-4 record as a member of the USA National Team for seven years, including winning a gold medal and a silver medal in the Olympics. (Photo courtesy USA Softball)

Chapter 4

CAT OSTERMAN
"STRIKEOUT ARTIST"

Growing Smarter

Her full name is Catherine Leigh Osterman, but softball fans around the world simply know her as Cat. She was born in Houston, Texas and although she's been around the world as a softball player and ambassador for the game, doesn't stray far from her home state. Winning pitchers come in all shapes and sizes, but strikeout artists have to have something extra that forces the batter to completely miss the pitch. Once the pitcher lets go of the ball, where it will wind up can be determined by its speed, the direction it is traveling in and the axis and rate of spin. One extra rotation of the ball between the pitcher's release point and home plate can be the difference between a sharp breaking pitch or its easier-to-hit line-drive-producing cousin. Everything else being equal, the pitcher with the decided edge will be the one who can master the additional ball rotation. It is a matter of physics and human mechanics.

Cat Osterman describes herself as "lanky." Michele Smith tells the tale of how Cat was four inches shorter than Michele when they first met but four inches taller than Michele (6 feet 2 inches to Michele's 5 feet 10 inches) when Cat had fully grown.

Career Highlights
(Pitcher)

- *Led University of Texas to three appearances in NCAA Women's College World Series*
- *Compiled record of 136 wins & 25 losses with 2,265 strikeouts in 1,105.2 innings*
- *Ranks second in NCAA in Strikeouts, 6th in wins and first in strikeout average per seven innings (14.34)*
- *Hurled 85 shutouts in college, 20 no-hitters and 10 perfect games*
- *Big 12 Pitcher of the Year four times*
- *Four-time NFCA All-American (1 2nd team in 2002, 3 1st teams in 03, 05, 06)*
- *2005 & 2006 ESPY Award Winner*
- *2005-06 Honda Award Winner*
- *Named Big 12 Pitcher of the week 25 times*
- *Is only one of three college pitchers to have 2,000 strikeouts in career*
- *Three-time USA Softball College Player of the Year, 2003, 2005, 2006*
- *2007 graduate of Texas, psychology major*
- *Named third team Academic All-American in 2003*
- *Named first team ASA All-American in 2001*
- *Named third team ASA All-American in 1999*

What nobody contradicts is that Cat is blessed with long fingers, and it is long fingers that encourage tight ball rotation under the right tutelage. If you turn back to the opening picture, you can see that the fingers, along with the rest of her body, have done their job and she is ready for whatever will happen next. Look back at Cat's face and you will recognize the fully engaged intensity that each of these players brought to nearly every pitch of every game. Strikeout artists expect strikeouts and Cat was the best pitcher who ever played college fast pitch softball from a standpoint of average strikeouts per seven innings.

To better understand Cat Osterman, one should be aware that the best teams either came out of California, Arizona, or Connecticut. Texas championships went back to the days of two Texas A&M teams in the mid '80s. The relevance of that information comes later. Before that, the lanky Cat had to decide whether she wished to take her athletic career in the direction of basketball or softball. Through high school she hoped that she could do both.

Great athletes with parents who consider effort more important than wins or losses have the best chance of getting through their school age years with their love of sports intact. Cat's father, Gary, is described that way. As she told me, "Growing up, my dad was always preaching, if I was going to do something I was going to do it 100%. I did this in everything I did. I was a goalie in soccer and I dedicated myself to that position just like pitching. I had goal keeping lessons before or after team meetings. I had the same approach to pitching."

Cat's dad also supplied some insulation between his precocious daughter and the potential stresses of unrealistic high expectations for her by being there during important games. As she says, "My dad has been at almost every important game of my career, and I give him a fist pump before and after my games."

Cat learned the basics of a work ethic and pitching from

her father. "On my 11th birthday he gave me a pitching lesson with Tim Timmons in Houston. Dad sat on a bucket to catch me from then until well into my college career. He didn't make me do anything I didn't want to. He supported my career, but pushed me to be as good as possible daily. When we were going to Florida for a family trip, he thought out the idea of maybe trying to get in touch with Michele Smith. My dad has been the rock through everything. He's why I became the pitcher I am.

"Along with my dad is Ken Eriksen. He has been a big part of my life and career as well. It's at his camp that I met Michele for the first time, and he's been a second father to me for many years. I also have trusted him with my career since we both joined the USA program in 2001. Eriksen is a huge part of my career, especially post college.

"Michele Smith also provided a few lessons during my career. She became a mentor and often emailed my mom and dad to keep up to date on how I was doing. Michele has been someone I can talk to about many different aspects of our sport and the life we live. I'll forever be indebted to her for not only giving some lanky kid the time of day, not only for spending a few hours to give me lessons, but also for giving me something to aspire to be, both on and off the field."

Cat starred in Cypress Springs High School striking out 1,158 batters in 507 innings (1999-2001) but she was still unsure of whether basketball or softball was best for her. However, she describes a decisive turning point in her choice. "In the summer of 2000, the USA National Team was on their Central Park to Sydney Tour and my travel team, the Katy Cruisers, played them in an exhibition game in Fort Worth, Texas. I pitched five innings of one hit ball with 11 strikeouts. I think this type of outing led me to realize my future was with pitching, not jump shots." During that game, Cat faced Michele, who was one of the USA team's better hitters. "I was nervous when I struck her out the first time. I wasn't sure if it was okay to be excited." But she wasn't too nervous to do her job and eleven strikeouts in five innings against this team meant that Cat could be on the same field with anybody and do her job.

The Katy Cruisers, her ASA travel team, generated a few highlights around this time as well. In 2000 and 2001 the Cruisers took the Gold National Championships. As Cat describes it, "We were the first non-California team to win the Gold Nationals and we were the first team to ever win back-to-back titles. It was awesome to go there and win. It was my first real experience winning something that mattered. I can still remember the last out of the 2000 Nationals, a grounder to me."

When it came to choosing a college, the Texan, who derived so much satisfaction being the underdog from the Southwest, decided that she would continue that role for the Longhorns. She could have had a better chance to win National titles if she had chosen one of the powerhouse schools, but when you can reliably strike out over 14 batters in a seven inning game, you make any team you are on instantly competitive. It's also a guess that the fearless gunslinger mentality is shared by both Cat and Michele and part of the reason they are so fond of one another.

In Cat's 2002 freshman year she set University of Texas single season records with 51 appearances, 36 wins, 304 innings pitched, 40 games started. She established an NCAA freshman record of 554 strikeouts, pitched the Longhorn's first three perfect games and broke a number of strikeouts-per-inning standards. Between February 13th and March 13th she pitched 79 innings without giving up an earned run, which is also a UT record.

In 2003 Cat did double duty for the Longhorns in the spring and the USA team during the summer. She set career UT records in the following categories: wins (68); strikeouts (1,042) shutouts (35) and opponents' batting average (.105). Instead of earned runs, she has moved up to the category of shutout innings where she set a mark of 65 scoreless innings. Her strikeouts-per-game (14.1) has also set a new national record.

That summer Cat joined the USA team and, in the Pan American Games, pitched a perfect game against Team Canada in the gold medal game, winning 4-0. She took a leave of absence from UT and spent most of the next year preparing for the 2004 Olympics. The prep for the Olympics was very one-sided for their 53 game schedule and it continued right through the Olympic Games. Cat had two wins and a save for the gold medal team with 23 strikeouts.

Grace Under Pressure

How do you return from the Olympics energized to play your junior year of Division I college softball? For many it would be a difficult task, and that is what happened to Cat. "After coming home from the Athens Olympics I was burnt out. We had been on tour day in day out. The routine repeated itself daily and ended in Athens with a great finish. This made jumping right back to school and fall ball a grind. I needed help from Coach Connie Clark and my teammates to get through it. Eventually the feeling of it being a grind no longer lingered."

She considers this period of her life an important life lesson. "Through softball I have an extended family that I'm very thankful for. I have plenty of sisters across the country I know I can count on. When I was eighteen I had no idea what was in store for me. It took a long while for me to develop patience to understand how to be grateful for the opportunity presented to me."

"Everything that comes with being successful is hard to comprehend if you aren't prepared for it. It took me a while to grasp that. Now I can see the light in the little kids' eyes after games and understand their excitement. I still have my moments, but if softball has taught me anything, it is to be gracious, to love the life I've been given, and, more importantly, to share this sport and my passion for it with others."

In 2005 Cat again did double duty with UT and the USA team, continuing to break existing strikeout records. She finished her junior year with an average of 15.2 strikeouts per seven innings. In one seven inning game she struck out 19, two short of the maximum possible. During this year she was voted 2005 Sportswoman of the Year (team category) by the Women's Sports Foundation. In August of that year she made her TV debut as a color commentator for ESPN.

During her senior year she won her final NCAA career win (136) for 6th place all-time. In the WCWS she struck out a total of 18 in a 2-0 record setting performance. Her team never won the WCWS crown, but she did put UT on the map.

Grace Under Pressure can also be measured by how someone handles defeat. Cat was on the mound the day the USA lost in the 2008 Olympiad in Beijing to Japan in the gold medal game. Until that game the USA team had won 22 consecutive games. Osterman's performance up until that time, three wins and a save, had earned her the ball for this game. She pitched the first five innings in a 3-1 loss to Japan and has described at least one pitch that she would like to have back. Sometimes defeat can mark a lesser player or person. Cat has been forthright about the game and the tournament and has put it behind her. That is a key way that she retains her poise in a world quick to forget the positives and focus on the negatives.

Since the Olympics Cat has broadened her perspective by doing Division I Assistant coaching and continuing to play pro ball in the U.S. This past spring she followed mentor Michele Smith's example by playing in the Japan Softball League.

Doing Good by Being Good

When Cat began playing International softball for the USA team she was one of its younger players. There were people with whom she developed a strong bond. Now, she is the icon that others look up to and she takes her responsibilities seriously. When asked, "how has that changed your life?" she had this to say: "The biggest thing is that I had to adapt as a person myself because I'm playing softball. It's what I do including everything else that came with it. I didn't expect the fan attention. I just wanted to play softball in college and see where it took me.

"Having to be aware of your personality and sometimes adjust it is not easy. Sometimes after a loss you don't want to sign autographs or even smile, but you have to find a way to do it. It was hard for me for a long time. I had to figure out at a young age how to adapt to all of that. I think it made me grow up really fast because I started with the National team out of high school and had to mature as a player and a person faster than most people do in the game. Would I change it? No, I wouldn't change it for anything. I've enjoyed everything softball has given me."

To give emphasis to that point, in early August, 2011, St Edward's University, a Division II school in Austin, Texas, announced that former Texas infielder Lindsay Gardner would be taking on softball head coaching duties for the school next year supported by her teammate, Cat Osterman. Osterman and Gardner have played together a number of times, starting with travel squads and moving to UT and Pro ball. The team is excited.

Pitcher Cat Osterman compiled a won-loss record of 136-25 during her four years at the University of Texas, leading the Longhorns to three NCAA Women's College World Series appearances.
(Photo courtesy University of Texas Athletics)

College softball's Sultan of Swat, Stacey Nuveman, smashed 90 homers during her career at UCLA. (Photo courtesy UCLA Sports Information)

Chapter 5

STACEY NUVEMAN
"AWESOME POWER"

Grace Under Pressure

Stacey Nuveman has a very friendly, inviting smile and manner – that is, until she gets between the lines. Look at either the picture to the left, supplied with the permission of UCLA Sports Information, or the photo in the color section, and you will have no doubt that the competition, at this moment, is not fun and games. It is serious business. There is something primal happening between that stick and stone. As you observe Stacey's shoulders and hips pulling around the fulcrum of her left leg with her eyes focused on the spot near where the ball made contact with her bat, and that same bat completing a full swing, two things are likely to occur to you: first, her great balance and power; second, the hope that whoever was in front of that missile had time to get her glove between herself and her exposed body.

This book could have been called "Dreams and Nightmares" because so many of the profiles drawn here are about the dreams of the players who had early aspirations to be the best player they could be. After seeing the picture on the left, imagine being on the left side of the infield after the barrel of the bat has made line drive contact. That is the stuff of which nightmares

43

Career Highlights
(Catcher, First Base)

• Member of 2000, 2004 and 2008 USA Olympic softball team
•Gold medalist in 2000 and 2004; Silver medalist in 2008
•NCAA career leader in homers (90), slugging percentage (.945)
•Second all-time in NCAA career batting average (.466)
•In 264 NCAA games, drove in 299 runs, had 653 total bases,
      240 walks and 81 intentional walks
•Career on-base percentage was .600
•Is one of only five players to bat at least .400, drive in
      200 runs, and hit 50 homers
•Led NCAA in total bases twice, 1999 (187) and 2002 (164)
•Led NCAA in slugging percentage in 2002 (1.045)
•Named USA College Softball Player of the Year, 2002
•Member of ISF World Championship Teams 2002 and 2006
•Gold Medalist for Pan American Games qualifier, 2005
•Silver medalist at Japan Cup, 2005
•Silver Medalist at 2005 World Cup, batted .429 with four
      RBI and two homers
•Gold Medalist at 1999 and 2003 Pan American Games
•Batted .409 with nine RBIs and three runs scored at 2002
      ISF World Championship
•Gold Medalist at U.S. Cup, 2001
•Assistant at San Diego State 2009-2010
•Assistant Head Coach, San Diego State 2011
•2011 named to USA Coaching Pool

are born, and you can guess that Stacey inspired many a night of tossing and turning before an opposing player could sleep. One thing they would not have had to concern themselves about, however, would be the threat of the bunt or the walk. Opponents considered giving her a pass to first base an acceptable way to keep that swing from dumping another blast into the bleachers. If she walked or bunted, in most situations the other team would applaud.

Also, since Stacey Nuveman had four of the five tools (she was not fleet of foot), the opposing team could play back a bit and know that they had more time to throw her out. A little later we will get into Nuveman's incomparable batting statistics, but we'll start with the fact that for every ten times Stacey Nuveman came to the plate, she got on base six of them, for a college career .600 on-base-percentage. Remember that she didn't get cheated when she took a rip, so these were not bloopers over the second baseman's head that dropped in. Every time she came up, the ball had a real chance to go out.

This part of the book is centered in the modern era, after the pitcher's mound was moved back to 43 feet in 1988 and the optic yellow ball (a replica of which is on the cover) replaced the white. So far you have read about pitchers who could hit and a speedster who fully rounded out her game. Here we come to a new character in the arsenal of the game, the awesome, primal-fear-invoking clean-up hitter. See that swing once and there is no question about her intent.

Stacey is often compared to former Major League Baseball player Mark McGwire, in part because they went to sister Catholic schools in California and because there is no mistaking that full swing that power hitters of both genders command. There might be some who would be offended by comparing Nuveman to McGwire, but not Stacey herself.

She had this to say to USA reporter David Leon Moore

around the time when she caught up to the all-time college career home run record (90): "I particularly enjoyed McGuire," she says, "I read a couple of articles with him talking about all the things he's thinking before he steps into the box vs. when he gets in there to hit. When he gets into the box, he's not thinking about anything. He's just looking at the release point. As a hitter, that's beautiful to hear that kind of thing, to see that absolute focus and concentration, that kind of peaceful calm that he has before absolutely ripping a 500 foot bomb. I feel I've learned from that."

Grace Under Pressure can be found in that sequence: The initial calm which provides maximum readiness for the subsequent action, followed by the storm and its quick, lightning violence. Too much thinking slows down reaction time, but too much uncoordinated violence in the action robs the result of power. Balance these features as Nuveman had and you have the swing that interferes with a pitcher's good night sleep.

Stacey was one of the young and gifted players given the opportunity to play full-time with Team USA, taking a leave of absence from UCLA between her sophomore and junior years to do so. Because of the way she could hit, she was in a position to be the signal-caller for an experienced group of pitchers that included Lisa Fernandez (one of her assistant coaches at UCLA) and Michele Smith (a veteran international pitcher) in 2000. She describes a difficult transition: from being a player told by the coach how things are supposed to be done to a catcher expected by the coach to take charge of letting the pitchers know how the pitches are moving and what can be done to throw them better. Politeness and deference may be very helpful off the field, but those traits have nothing to do with communicating how to best get out of a one-pitch-away jam. It's not just about knowing what to do, it is about communicating with confidence so the pitcher throws the pitch with full effort whether the catcher is right or wrong. Better to be wrong with conviction than be right without confidence.

Here is how Stacey remembers that 2000 Olympic group: "Playing on the 2000 team was very humbling for me because I was a rookie, the youngest player on the team, and being asked to catch Lisa Fernandez, Michele Smith, Lori Harrigan and other veterans I had always looked up to. I remember Lisa telling me early on, during one of our bullpen sessions, that she wanted me to give her feedback on what I was seeing, mechanically and otherwise. I was intimidated by her, needless to say, and could not imagine me giving Lisa Fernandez feedback/coaching. Eventually, I got over that intimidation and we had very good rapport. It was the same for my relationship with Smitty and Harrigan.

"I always say that catching is two parts sports psychologist and one part catcher, and I took great pride in my ability to get to know each pitcher individually and learning how I could help them to be at their best. I may not have always been the best physical catcher, but I think my pitchers liked throwing to me and they believed I called a good game for them."

Growing Smarter

Relatively speaking, it is most likely that from her earliest coaches, beginning with Larry Mays and the Gordon Panthers, through Sue Enquist at UCLA and Ralph Raymond with the 2000 Olympic team, nobody said very much to her about how to swing a bat at a ball. I'm sure they encouraged her to "pick out a good one, and give it a rip," or some such cheer you make when you are thanking your lucky stars that she plays for you and not them.

For effect, let's throw in some statistics to consider (they don't include typos – we have been particularly careful because the stats are that special). NCAA career record in homers (90), second in career batting average (.466) In 264 games she drove in 299 runs, had 653 total bases, 240 walks and 81 intentional walks. Stacey is only one of five players to bat at least .400, drive in 200 runs and hit 50 home runs. Let's look at that again. Only five players batted at least .400 (She hit .466), drove in 200 runs (she drove in 299) and hit 50 home runs (she hit 90). In 2002, she led the NCAA in slugging percentage (1.045)

Some of her other batting stats and honors and awards are found on page 44 on the second page of this chapter. They are worth looking at. But this is a section on growing smarter, and that's where Stacey Nuveman's ability to grow into her catching position to become a positive defensive force for both the 2000 and 2004 Olympic Gold Medal teams and the 2008 Silver Medal team is so important.

Here's what Stacey had to say about each of the four pitchers profiled in this book who she caught in the 2000 and 2004 Olympics, Fernandez, Smith, Finch, and Osterman: "I don't think Lisa had a true-blue best pitch. And I honestly think that's what made her so successful. She had so many great pitches that she could go to, on any given day. She could reinvent herself on the mound every time out and she never became predictable."

"Smitty was mostly up and down, which I think is somewhat of a lost art in today's game. Cat is the same way. Of course they complimented their drop and rise with off-speed and such, but at the end of the day they both changed planes exceptionally well. Smitty had more speed and Cat's movement is off the charts. To this day, and even before Cat came on the scene, I have never seen a drop ball that moved as much as Cat's. It is the true definition of 'off the table.'

"Finch was more of a power pitcher, and she used a lot of in/out. She relied a lot on location, and she understood the value and importance of 'getting it in on the hands.' She was not afraid to throw up and in, and then mix outside. She was the master of the mix and knew how to use all of her weapons."

Listening to Stacey differentiate between these "best of the best" should give you a clear idea of how the tuned-in catcher, who knows how each pitcher performs at her best, can rate today's effort against an average day, a good day, or a bad day. Nearly anybody with the right reflexes can catch a good to great pitcher on a good day. Put the target somewhere, call the pitch and be ready for it to hit the target. It's a game of pitch and catch. It is on days when something is not working that the "two part psychologist" and "one part catcher" must go to work. Stacey has a sociology degree from UCLA, so she knows full well that the catcher's job is to be full of whatever that pitcher needs to find what's missing. For some it will be a temporary loss of focus, for others a mechanical mix-up. Nuveman's job is to make that pitcher enjoy throwing to her so she can take advantage of gaining experience in how to help them be at their best.

By 2004, Mike Candrea thought so much of Stacey's signal-calling skills that she called her own games. On Candrea, Stacey remarks: "He's such a father figure. His dedication, his presence, his focus and commitment really wore off on me. It had a pretty huge effect on my playing the game at this level and respecting it as well."

Doing Good by Being Good

Stacey Nuveman is a firm believer in paying the game back. She knows that she has had about the best set of coaching talent that anyone could ask for and has tried to take something from everybody, as in the example above regarding Coach Candrea.

It started with her family who she credits with "being instrumental in giving me the opportunity to pursue the game and my dream of taking the game to the highest level." Coach Larry Mays "was a great influence in my career at really looking at the game from every possible angle." Sue Enquist "was the ultimate motivator, life lessons, accountability and responsibility; things you really have to have to move on to the national and Olympic level."

She specifically remembers the 2000 Olympic Games, when the team came all the way back after losing three tough match-ups. "I feel very fortunate to have had the opportunity to play for Coach Ralph Raymond. He's obviously very old school and a very simple coach. He didn't over-analyze. Playing for Coach Raymond was very special."

Consistent with her philosophy of giving something back to the game, Stacey Nuveman has been an assistant for two years at San Diego State before being named assistant head coach in 2011. She was married to Mark Deniz in 2003 and has a four-year-old son, Chase Gregory Deniz.

Stacey can also be found working with several non-profit organizations, including Visalia Miracle League, the Women's Sports Foundation and the Make-a-Wish Foundation.

This past June, Stacey's home run record was within three of being broken. Now that she is on the "give back" side of the game, we can expect her to enjoy the news of that accomplishment whenever it is earned. Until then, she enjoys the crown of Softball's Sultan of Swat.

You might not have known this, but in high school Stacey Nuveman served as student body president. Even then, she understood the value of being part of something that she could help make better.

A threat to send the softball out of the park every time she batted, Nuveman finished second all-time in NCAA career batting average (.466) and was a member of three USA Olympic teams. (Photo courtesy USA Softball).

*USA National Team pitcher Jennie Finch high fives teammate Natasha Watley
(Photo USA Softball)*

Chapter 6

JENNIE FINCH
"GOODWILL AMBASSADOR"

Doing Good by Being Good

Jennie Finch is the perennial "fan favorite" player of women's softball. She is also a person who carried (and continues to carry) herself with a consistent grace on and off the ball field. Her player statistics hold up through a national and international career that started when she was about 12 and continued through her retirement at 29 during the summer of 2010. At least from the time she was crowned best college player in the nation in 2001 to her final days in the game, she carried a dual identity: a champion with a fierce desire to win and a "crossover representative" of the sport.

It is her "crossover" characteristics that are being highlighted under "Doing Good by Being Good" because Jennie came to softball prominence at a time when the game was rapidly growing in popularity – she is given credit by fast-pitch insiders for understanding how critical her contribution could be to the acceptance and growth of their favorite sport.

Compared to its current status, women's softball started in relative obscurity. Its most influential leaders worked mostly

Career Highlights

(Pitcher, First Base)

- 2001, 2002 – Honda Award Winner as nation's top college softball player.
- 2001 – Led U of Arizona to Women's College World Series title
- 2002 – Named to WCWS All-Tournament Team
- 1999-2002 – Compiled 119-16 record at U of Arizona, for .881 winning percentage.
- 2001 – had an unbeaten college season, 32-0
- 2000-2002 won a record 60 games in a row (continues as record)
- 2000 and 2001 Won ASA National titles with Phoenix Storm
- 1998 – Gold Medalist at the USA Softball Women's National Team Festival
- 1997 – ASA 18-under Gold National Champions with Orange County Batbusters
- 2002 and 2006 –Two time World Champion
- 2003 and 2007 – Two-time Pan Am gold medalist
- 2004 – Olympic gold medalist
- 2008 – Olympic silver medalist.
- 1995 – Won ASA 14-under National Championship (California Cruisers)
- 1993 – Won ASA 12-under National Championship (California Cruisers)
- Pitched 6 years in NPF before announcing retirement following 2010 season.

behind the scenes to get proper fields, fair allocation of government funding, and a reasonable measure of fan interest and support. In the early '80s, with the implementation of Title IX, a piece of Congressional legislation that assures equal funding for male and female subsidized programs, a number of dedicated workers put the modern game together at the college level. The NCAA Women's College World Series (WCWS) has steadily grown in popularity since the early days. In the mid 1980's you could expect a crowd of about 1,000 or fewer for games. This year's WCWS championship game was played before more than 6,000.

The game received a second boost when it was added to the Olympic roster in 1996. Jennie was an important contributor to both the 2004 and 2008 teams, playing a key role in crucial victories for each USA Team. But for Jennie there were so many requests from media sources to be where the camera could take advantage of her photogenic abilities that it is my guess for her the ball field could become a refuge from paparazzi, reporters, and interviewers. Not that Jennie Finch complained or refused to be helpful in the interest of furthering the popularity of the game. She clearly understood that the press creates celebrities, puts them on pedestals, and waits patiently for something embarrassing to happen which can turn into provocative grist for the public imagination. She was determined that she would not put herself or her sport in an embarrassing or compromising position, and for her entire career she has been a beacon of keeping true to herself while not turning popularity into notoriety.

I had a chance to chat with Jennie in 2006 when she was selected to the 25th Anniversary College Team. The festivities were hosted by the ASA Hall of Fame in Oklahoma City and the atmosphere was bright and cheerful. Jennie had completed her storied college career, which included one championship and two Honda Awards as the best player in her sport. She was a recent Gold Medal Olympian and a fixture of the USA Team. Her crossover resume by that time also included appearing in the swimsuit edition of *Sports Illustrated* and being one of People Magazine's "50 Most Beautiful People." She was accomplished, competitive and beautiful. How, I wondered, would she be to talk to?

The answer was immediate and consistent with her reputation. She was down-to-earth and genuine – in other words, "the real deal." The amount of publicity and exposure had not affected her as much as other athletes would have been affected. We had a pleasant conversation about softball and I went away pleased that our most visible and quoted spokesperson had made such a favorable impression.

Sometime later, I was walking through the Hall of Fame when I spotted Jennie with a group of 30 to 40 young girls. Their attention was fully riveted on her and everyone was having a great time. Everyone wanted something from Jennie, an autograph for a hat (or whatever they could think of to get her to sign) or a photograph to permanently mark the occasion. Whatever they wanted, Jennie was patient and accommodating. Like all celebrities who understand their impact on fans, she did her best to provide a set of special moments, including words of encouragement to work hard and aim high. It was obvious that a number of young women had established a bond with a very famous player who valued representing the game as an attractive way to spend quality time.

There is another part of Jennie Finch's message to young girls that has had the effect of expanding more girls' interest in the game. Jennie had popularized feminine glitter and decorative headbands. Obviously she doesn't believe that her game should be without a feminine fashion statement. Glitter is now accepted in more and more places as an appropriate uniform accessory.

Sixty years ago, women were expected to look feminine so

as not to offend people who didn't think that it was proper for a woman to get dirty or sweaty. The result was a uniform that made playing the game uncomfortable and sliding somewhat dangerous. Over the next fifty years the pendulum swung and women's uniforms took on the same long legged utility as men's. Women were able to shed the demand to adapt uncomfortable outfits to satisfy others. Jennie Finch came along and expanded the idea of what is acceptable for a woman to wear on the field. No one is prescribing what women must do, rather there is an expansion of possibilities. This is consistent with messages that top ball players have given younger women – you can be anything you want to be, and no one else defines your limits.

In an article (http:www.usatoday.com/sports/Olympics/ 2010-07-26-finch-closes-out) in USA Today, her college and Olympic Coach Mike Candrea had this to say: "I think sometimes you measure a person's success not on their accomplishments as much as how many lives they've touched…Jennie has transformed this sport, touched millions of kids in many different ways – whether it's fashion, whether it's the way she plays the game – but through it all she's been humble…She's become the face of this sport, and not many people could do that…It's hard to do."

Grace Under Pressure

During the media buzz surrounding Jennie's first Olympics in 2004, she demonstrated Grace Under Pressure repeatedly by sticking to her convictions that softball is a team sport and should celebrate team-focused contributions. Reporters and interviewers tried as many ways as they could think of to make it seem that she was somehow representing the USA all by herself. She would have none of that. Wherever possible, Jennie would mention the teamwork aspects of her sport while she identified just how accomplished and attractive her seventeen teammates were. Her elevating and supporting the other members of her team felt genuine and necessary, and she did it without getting rattled or visibly annoyed. She was speaking from a position of deepest respect for what it takes to be the best of the best.

There is another situation that comes to mind in which Jennie showed a proper balance of poise and self-respect. After winning an ESPN 2003 fan poll for "Most Beautiful Women Athlete," she was asked which was more important, to be considered beautiful or a champion. She made it clear that being considered an athlete who was beautiful was far less important than being an athlete who had been tested in her sport and been able to earn the title of champion.

Growing Smarter

The Jennie Finch sports story starts when she was five years old and began playing ball. She started pitching when she was 8, her first softball teacher being her father. Her mother and father, Doug and Bev Finch, were not dabblers when it came to their child's interest in sports. When she was 10 years old, according to the Finch Windmill Website, Jennie's father invented a machine to help his daughter and others who were learning the windmill motion develop their throwing muscles and keep both sides of their body more equally muscular. The Finch Windmill has been sold for 20 years. What seems noteworthy here is that Mr. Finch went one step beyond any parent that I am aware of by taking the time and effort to design something that could help reduce physical problems caused by the pitching motion. That represents an extremely high level of family dedication.

In 1992, at around the age of 12, Jennie's team came in 4th

in the 12-under ASA National Championship. A year later her team won the championship. This pattern was repeated during the next two years when her 14-under team came in 4th only to be followed the next year with a first place finish. Later, with her 18-under team she also won the ASA championship.

Jennie's high school career is similarly studded with impressive achievements. She compiled a 50-12 record with an ERA of 0.15 and 784 strikeouts in 445 innings pitched. She had 6 perfect games, 13 no-hitters and 14 one-hitters. She also played first base and shortstop. At the completion of her high school career *Jump* magazine selected her as the nation's top recruit (Material found on University of Arizona sports website).

One might assume that the jump from high school to college would have required some adjustments, but the record shows that in her freshman year Jennie came one victory short (she won 24) from tying the all-time freshman mark. When she didn't pitch she played first base. In the regionals she hit .353, pitched a no-hitter, a one hitter and a two hitter for NCAA Region 2 Most Outstanding player honors.

During her sophomore year she was 29-2 with a 0.79 ERA. She hit .327 with 16 home runs and once again led her team with a 3-0 record in the Regionals for her second Most Outstanding Player Award. Here is where, as with other career achievements, Jennie just keeps getting better with more experience.

In 2001, her junior year, she established an NCAA record by winning every game she pitched (32-0) including the WCWS. In the finals her team beat UCLA 1-0. She won her first Honda Award as the best player in college softball, was the Most Outstanding Player in the WCWS (3-0), had a season ERA of 0.54, and built a consecutive win streak of 40. In 2002 Jennie started the season by winning 20 consecutive games to set the current college record of 60 victories in a row. She won 34 games her senior year, and received her second Honda Award.

As has been noted, after college Finch was a very important player on the USA team. She was named to the 2004 Olympic team and had a 2-0 record helping the team capture the gold. In 2008 she again represented her country, giving up no runs in three appearances against Venezuela, Chinese Taipei, and China. She pitched a total of 7 innings. In the final game the USA lost to Japan and everyone expressed disappointment with the Silver Medal performance.

Jennie's retirement from softball coincides with the birth of Diesel (born June 19th, 2011), the second son of Finch and husband Casey Daigle (married January 15th, 2005), whose first son, Ace, was born May 4th, 2006. She leaves as a player at the top of her game, having been voted ASA Female Softball Athlete of the year in 2009. During her tenure as the most easily recognizable crossover athlete in softball history, she provided prodigious talent, fierce dedication and unwavering grace to her legacy. During the ceremonies that accompanied her departure as a player, her unique contributions to the game were remembered and appreciated. Jennie did it her way and the game is better off because of it.

In closing, this is what Ron Radigonda, ASA Executive Director, had to say about Jennie: "Jennie Finch is a 'Gold Medal Person.' She became an icon for the sport of softball and the most recognized player in the history of the game. Throughout her decade journey with ASA/USA Softball that encompasses two Women's World Championships, two Olympic Games and hundreds of cities in the United States, she was never too busy to sign an autograph or take a picture with a young fan."

Jennie Finch compiled a record of 119-16 at the University of Arizona including a record 60 consecutive wins and was a member of two USA Olympic teams. (Photo courtesy USA Softball)

Staring down the batter, Monica Abbott was the USA Softball Player of the Year in 2007 and a silver medalist on the 2008 Olympic Team. (Photo courtesy of USA Softball)

Chapter 7

MONICA ABBOTT
"TIRELESS FIREBALLER"

Grace Under Pressure

When Monica Abbott was ten years old she was on a team in California. Her coach, a guy named Keith Berg, was a dedicated softball mentor who took the time to go to clinics to learn as much as he could about the finer points of the game. Ralph Weekly was one of the presenters at the clinic, and after his presentation, Keith found himself in a position to ask Weekly questions about hitting.

Here is what Ralph Weekly remembers: "He wanted to talk to me about hitting, so I spent 45 minutes talking to him about hitting. And at that point I was an assistant on the National Olympic Team. I guess he was pretty impressed that a guy that was an assistant on the Olympic team would spend as much time with a guy coaching 10 year-olds. I am just happy to do it. I do this like everyone else involved. When I do clinics I spend a lot of time with the coaches. I was just fortunate that I struck up a conversation with him eight years before I even knew there was a Monica. And we kept in touch. Keith had told Monica that I was a good person and a good coach. I guess that helped out."

Ralph and Karen Weekly watched Monica play high school

Career Highlights
(Pitcher)

- 2007 USA Softball Player of the Year and Women's Sports Foundation Sportswoman of the Year
- Pitched Tennessee to third and second place finishes in WCWS
- Named to NCAA WCWS All-Tournament Team 2005, 06, 07
- Silver Medalist on 2008 USA Olympic Team
- Two-Time gold medalist in 2008 ISF World Championship 2006 and 2010
- Three-time gold medal in World Cup 2006, 2007, 20009
- Only player with more than one NCAA 50-win season (two)
- Only player with four NCAA 500 strikeout seasons and two 600 strikeout seasons
- 2007, Holds NCAA record for most strikeouts in a season – 724
- 2005, Holds NCAA record for most games pitched in a season – 69
- Most Wins (45) and most strikeouts (582) in a season by a freshman
- Holds NCAA career records for wins (189), strikeouts (2,440) shutouts (112), games (253), games started (206) and innings pitched (1,448). Is second in most complete games (178)
- Averaged 11.80 strikeouts per seven innings in college, third best all-time
- Has a career winning percentage of .848 with 189 wins and 34 losses
- Saved 16 games in college and hurled 23 no-hitters and 6 perfect games

ball her junior year and watched her play summer ball and knew they were in an intense recruitment rivalry with the best schools in the country. Asked how Monica selected Tennessee, Ralph initially pointed to the fact that Michele Granger, a tall (5'10"), hard thrower from California, had joined the Tennessee coaching staff. He also mentioned the connection that Karen was beginning to develop with Monica.

But in the end it was a visit to the campus during a game between UT and Florida with 108,000 people in the stands that clinched it for Monica. As Ralph Weekly remembers, "It's very impressive when you come to Tennessee on football weekend. We lost the game, it rained half the day, we fumbled about five times and I told Karen on our way back to the office, 'I don't think we'll ever get her now.' Karen said, 'You never know.'

"So the next Wednesday, Monica called us and said, 'I want to come to Tennessee.' Of course I knew that was really going to help us establish a program. I knew as hard as we were working recruiting other kids that we could build this program for years to come. I ask her why and she said, 'I went to a football game. There were 108,000 people there in orange. It rained, Tennessee lost, nobody left and everybody kept cheering for Tennessee right to the end. And that made me know that's where I wanted to go.'"

According to Monica: "I knew Ralph and Karen and I knew they were going to have an up-and-coming program. I knew their reputation as coaches and their desire for success, but the biggest thing I wanted was to go to a school that loved their athletes. A school like Tennessee. Not only do they love their athletes, but they love their female athletes even more."

"That's what she told the San Francisco papers, too," Weekly says. "I think the primary thing was that she knew how great UCLA was and she knew the legacy of UCLA, but she also wanted to go somewhere where she could strike a path. She said that to me many times. She wanted to blaze a trail, and she did.

Without her, the Sherri Parker Lee Softball Stadium wouldn't have been built, and we probably have the most beautiful stadium in the country. It's about $12 million and we call it 'The House that Monica Built.'

"The other thing about Monica is that she was very humble over her entire career. Everybody in Tennessee loves her. She is one of the few people that people know who you're talking about if you say her first name. In Tennessee, Pat Summit (UT Head Basketball Coach) is on a level above everyone else, but Monica Abbott is also pretty well-loved in the state of Tennessee. Monica was never a prima donna. She was the key to getting where we are now. She got involved in all kinds of activities on campus and got heavily involved with the Fellowship of Christian Athletes. Monica was a little bit shy and a little bashful about things when she came to UT. By the time she left she was a gifted speaker and very polished."

Here is how Monica remembers it: "I think the biggest jump for me was more mental than physical. Dealing with more mature people, much more mature athletes. Also having to adjust to being away from home and having a lot of personal responsibility. I was very young and started out very, very shy because of my role as pitcher. I wasn't yet good at communicating. I really wasn't used to speaking my opinion. I really didn't know my own voice. Ralph and Karen helped me figure that out."

Growing Smarter

Part of Monica's growth process as a pitcher was through her work with Michele Granger. "She was there to challenge me. The most important thing Michele Granger ever told me was, 'Monica, you throw hard. Other pitchers throw slow. When you throw slow the ball has lots of movement, when you throw hard you have no movement. Why not have both?' And that always stuck with me."

Her philosophy about pitching is that there's always something new to learn. "I always feel there are areas of improvement. I would like to develop more off-speed. I have an off-speed, how much slower do you want to go? You can always pinpoint the drop better, get it to fall off the table more, read hitters better."

Growing up, Monica's parents were her biggest influence. "My mom (Julie) caught for me every day and my dad (Bruce) taught me about life and the world. He is my beacon of information. I can bounce anything off him and get an honest reply back." Monica Abbott attended North Salinas High School in Salinas, California as both a softball and basketball player. There are paragraphs of honors that she received during her high school years but suffice it to say that she was named all-state, all-county and all-league in both basketball and softball. She received the Cal-Hi Softball Athlete of the Year, the Sports Focus Athlete of the Year, the state large school player of the year, and the MVP trophies for her high school, conference, county and section (source: U Tenn). She was named Athletic Player of the Year and Athlete of the Year and received Prep Female Athlete of the Year honors from the Monterey Bay Herald and the San Jose Mercury News.

Her choice of the University of Tennessee was an immediate success for both player and team. She made the Louisville Slugger/NFCA First Team All-American. Abbott finished her freshman year, 45-10, had a 1.03 ERA with 44 complete games in 59 appearances. She had four no-hitters and a perfect game while striking out 582 batters in 352 innings. Abbott also holds the distinction of being the first Lady Vol to be considered as a finalist for USA Softball's Collegiate Player of the Year. She even became the first pitcher in NCAA history to strike out 500 in a season, repeating that feat every season for Tennessee.

During Monica's four years as a Volunteer, Tennessee played 297 games and she pitched all but 44 of them. The team's records were 55-16, 67-15, 61-12, and 63-8. The subject of that massive amount of work was brought up with Coach Weekly, who said, "First of all, if you've got a player that is 6'3," very, very strong, very durable, and she wants the ball, you would be stupid not to give it to her. I always told Monica, 'If you have any twitch, any pain, anything at all, let me know and I will take you out.' But Monica wanted the ball because she had goals. And Monica's goals were to seek the strikeout record, seek the number of wins record…Like I said, if the pitcher is healthy and wants the ball, I don't think any coach in the country wouldn't give it to her."

Joan Joyce was called the Big Train by Brakette Coach Ralph Raymond because she wanted the ball all the time like Walter Johnson. "We had a nickname for Monica kind of similar to that at Tennessee. We called her the Big Unit, after Randy Johnson. That was her nickname at Tennessee. There were days when Monica said, 'Coach, I don't feel well today,' and I wouldn't throw her – I make up the lineup. She was one in a million, and that kind of kid doesn't come along that often."

During that four year span as a member of the Lady Volunteers, she became college softball's all-time strikeout leader with 2,440 strikeouts in 1,448 innings. The strikeouts and innings pitched are the most in NCAA history, as are career wins (189), shutouts (112), games (253) and games started (206). Angela Tincher, Cat Osterman and Monica Abbott are the only pitchers with 2,000 strikeouts or more.

Abbott was the only player to have earned at least forty wins in each of her four seasons and the only player to have won fifty games in two seasons. Abbott was also the only player to have played four seasons with 500 or more strikeouts and the only player to get 600 in at least two. In one of those seasons she struck out 724 batters, the most ever in a single season. In 2005, she pitched 69 games, the most ever pitched in a season.

Monica says that breaking the career strikeout record and

leading Tennessee to the WCWS for the first time are two of the highlights of her career. During her sophomore, junior, and senior years, she led her school to two third place finishes and one second place finish. In 2005, she beat Arizona 1-0, lost to UCLA 3-1, beat Alabama 4-0 and lost to Michigan 3-2. Tennessee finished third in the tournament.

In 2006 she defeated UCLA, then lost to Northwestern (2-0). She then defeated Arizona State University 3-1 in nine innings, defeated Arizona 1-0 in seven, and lost to Arizona 6-0 in seven innings, finishing third in the tournament.

In 2007 she pitched an opening game no-hitter with 16 strikeouts to beat Texas A&M 2-0. She then beat Arizona 1-0 in seven innings while giving up six hits, no runs, and three walks, striking out sixteen batters. In the third game against Northwestern, she won 3-0 in seven innings, giving up two hits and no walks with seventeen strikeouts. This was followed by a 3-0 victory over Arizona in seven innings with four hits and eight strikeouts. In the championship game she lost to Arizona 1-0 in ten innings, with the run being unearned, and eleven strikeouts. Tennessee left fourteen runners on base. She lost the "if" game 5-0 in six innings, giving up five earned runs. Tennessee left twelve runners on base and finished in second place in the tournament.

Doing Good by Being Good

When Monica Abbott joined the Lady Volunteers she knew that it would be an uphill battle to get her team over the top in just four years. Her outstanding record, particularly in her senior year, suggests that the best pitcher in that tournament was not the one who took home first prize. But her gallantry was in carrying a team, a school, and a state on her broad shoulders and taking them as close as you can get to the prize without taking it home.

Monica's All-World post college international career is almost anticlimactic in that she is no longer the only ace on the staff and can expect a breather from time to time. As a member of the USA National Team, she compiled a 13-1 record with 125 strikeouts in 71 innings. She was a silver medalist in the 2008 Olympic Games, a two-time gold medalist in the ISF World Championships (2006 & 2010, a three-time gold medalist in the World Cup (2006, 2007 and 2009) and an ASA first team All-American in 2005.

Recently, as a professional fast-pitch softball player around the world, she has led the Japan Softball League in strikeouts and ERA in 2010, hurled a perfect game in the Japan League Championship, and been named the Japan League MVP. Back in the United States, she was a 2010 All-NPF selection. At the time this piece is being written, her team, the Chicago Bandits, has just won the 2011 NPF Championship 10-3.

When asked about her future, Monica makes it clear that she believes she was put on this Earth to be a ballplayer. "My life will always be around softball and I am so blessed to be able to say that." The Weeklys say, "We can never repay Monica for all she's done for us, not just as a player but as a person."

This year we recognize Monica as the top professional pitcher in the world. It will be interesting to see where her talents, maturity, and dedication to the game take her in the years to come. Wherever that may be, we know that she will always have the appreciation and support of the fans in her adopted Volunteer state rooting actively for their Monica.

Monica Abbott put the University of Tennessee softball program on the map during her outstanding four years in Knoxville. (Photo courtesy UT Media Relations)

Dr. Dot Richardson was a member of two USA gold medal-winning teams, 1996 and 2000, and hit the game-winning homer in the 1996 gold medal game against China. (Photo courtesy USA Softball)

Chapter 8

Dot Richardson
"Dr. Dot"

Doing Good by Being Good

D
ot Richardson is a best-selling author, an Olympian on our first women's 1996 Olympic softball team, a physician, an orthopedic surgeon, an executive at a prestigious hospital overseeing the operations of a state-of-the-art sports, health & education campus, a wife, the NCAA's Player of the Decade for the '80's, a two-term Vice Chair of the President's Council on Physical Fitness and Sports, a member of the Governor's Council on Physical Fitness and a consistent champion of causes. But most of all she has this knack for having dreams and aspirations for herself and others that turn into real accomplishments.

Her bestselling 1997 book *Living the Dream*, takes us from the time she found out that there was such a thing as the Olympics to standing on the Gold Medal podium, where as a young girl she imagined herself. Between these retellings she relates tales of overcoming the limitations others placed on her. Their standards were typically too low and her exceptional skills were underestimated, but the belief in her passion coupled with

Career Highlights
(Shortstop, Second Base)

- 1996, 2000 Olympic Games Gold Medalist – hit game-winning homer in 1996
- NCAA Player of the Decade, 1980's
- 1980-83 three-time NCAA All-American UCLA
- 1980-83 three-time MVP, UCLA
- 1981 National Champions
- 15-time ASA All-American between 1970-2000
- Member of 10 ASA National Championship teams
- Seven-time winner of the Erv Lind Award as the top defensive player in the ASA
- 1999, 1995, 1987 and 1979 – Pan Am Games Gold Medalist, batted .318
- 1994, 1990, 1986 ISF World Championship – 3 gold medals
- 1983 Pan American Games Silver medalist
- Inducted into UCLA Athletic Hall of Fame in 1996
- Inducted into ASA Hall of Fame in 2006
- Member of the President's Council on Physical Fitness and Sports
- Graduate of UCLA (B.S. in kinesiology)
- Master's degree from Adelphi University
- Medical degree from Louisville Medical School
- Graduate of University of Southern Cal, orthopedic residency program
- Co-Founder & Commisioner – ProFastpitch X-treme Tour
- Fellowship of Christian Athletes – Softball Ministry – Board Chair

determination resulted in many dreams becoming reality.

What consistently comes across in her autobiography is an all-fired will to get where her talents and desires wanted to take her. What she was able to accomplish demonstrates that God-given gifts are meant to be shared no matter what obstacles we might face along the way. Dot was on an adult fast pitch softball team when she was only ten years old, a Women's Major Fast Pitch team when she was 13, and she made her first USA National team when she was 17. You really have to take your hat off to her mother and father for recognizing her gifts, trusting them and giving their support to her at a tender young age so that she can express her talents amongst older teammates and opponents.

Of course Dot knew that there was one thing that would become quickly apparent, she could play her position and her position was any place on the field that they chose to put her. During her illustrious career, she got the opportunity to play against many of the legends in the sport, like Sharron Backus, who recalls affectionately "that squirt" in right field, the 13-year-old rookie who seemed to run everything down plus make things happen with the stick. Facing one of the greatest pitchers of all time (Joan Joyce) for the first time, that squirt got a base hit up the middle and then quickly learned the true definition of athletic greatness when "the Legend" slammed the door shut for every remaining batter for the rest of the game.

Richardson goes back to the days when high school and junior high schools did not have fast pitch softball, only slow pitch. It was then a matter of showing off what the strong arm, the sure hands, the quick eye, and the swift feet could do, along with developing more control and pop in her swing. But even at a young age that isn't what stood out the most when talent evaluators looked at Dot Richardson. They saw a person brimming with confidence that could easily be distinguished from its less attractive relatives, arrogance or false modesty. Dot was, first and foremost, a player. Give her a chance to prove that and you were sure to forget just how young and inexperienced she was.

Dot had another characteristic that has never failed her: she is genuinely inspirational. From her first time in organized ball to the President's Council on Physical Fitness and Sports, she has the ability to connect to others and further everyone's goals. And that is independent of the size of the group – from one to ten thousand and one, it makes no difference. Dot's enthusiasm and commitment to noble causes generate tireless effort and a need to be part of something bigger than oneself. Another valuable character trait of Dot's is her faith. Do not look to her to throw in the towel if there is a glimmer of a hope to get something even a bit better. Who knows? From there, improvement might be contagious and cure might just be around the corner.

Living the Dream took us through the completion of the 1996 Olympics when Dr. Dot Richardson was performing a balancing act to fulfill her childhood dream of Olympic gold and becoming an orthopedic surgeon. The Olympic dream for Dot included having the first American hit, scoring the first run, becoming the first player to hit a home run in the modern Games (occurring during the first game against Puerto Rico in the sixth inning) and hitting the game-winning home run during the gold medal game against China. Literally hours after she and her teammates received the first ever Olympic Gold Medal in the sport of fast pitch softball, Dot was driven to the Today Show in Atlanta and then to the airport to fly back to Southern California to finish up her remaining three years at the USC Orthopedic Surgery Residency program. As has been pointed out, Dr. Dot Richardson has learned the art of behaving as a force of nature to be reckoned with. She is clear about what is on her "to do" list and the items are multi-tasked and not for the faint of heart. Yet, she is funny and likes to talk and makes you feel at home in her presence. We have had a number of conversations over the years and I have never had the sense that she was looking over my shoulder rushing to somewhere else. Even if we only have three minutes, Dr. Dot always knows how to maximize the sense of being humanly attached during the full three minutes.

During the days when she helped the Olympic cause by staying after games and talking to the fans, she had the ability to make each connection something the daughter and her parents could remember as encouraging and helpful for that child's aspirations. I know people 15 years later who can still feel what it was like for the daughter's heroine to supply positive words of encouragement; "Recognize the gifts God has given you and trust that those talents are meant to be shared. So remove all doubt and follow your passion to live your dreams regardless if others might think they are unobtainable. You are truly amazing!"

Growing Smarter

Right from the beginning, Dot Richardson was smart. You don't get an undergraduate degree at UCLA, with a B.S. in Kinesiology and Pre-med; a Master's in Exercise Physiology and Health at Adelphi University, a Medical Degree from the University of Louisville and an Orthopaedic Surgery Residency at the University of Southern California, followed by a Fellowship for the Kerlan-Jobe Orthopaedic Sports Medicine Clinic without being smart. But she was also smart in how she built a network of relationships throughout the country that helps her current programs thrive in a climate that would stop someone with less drive.

As a softball player, Dot Richardson had the advantage of sneaking up on her opponents. She seemed too small and too young to take seriously until the time when she drove one in the gap and wound up on third or hit one out. Her fundamental sense of the leadoff role was to get the party started; to set the tone of the game. When the leadoff hitter rips the ball off the bat, the opposing pitcher knows it's going to be a long day. "As the one hitter goes, so goes the rest of the team. As a leadoff batter, it is always best to start things off with conviction, commitment and confidence. Always start positively and make things happen quickly."

She knew that she would have to go to college out of state because her home state of Florida still did not offer fast pitch softball, only slow pitch. She also knew that she could not afford to go out of state for college unless she received financial assistance. Athletic scholarships had just begun to be given out to women only three years before and she knew this was her ticket to get a great education. She knew what an advantage it would be to attend a school that offered a degree in her field of interest, health care. She considered Texas A & M when she thought she might be interested in becoming a veterinarian, but she realized that her drive was to pursue athletic training or physical therapy or medicine. For her freshman year, she attended Western Illinois University, which had one of the most respected athletic training programs in the country. While there, she played field hockey, basketball, and softball. She led the nation with a .480 batting average and the team came in fifth in the country, but she realized that her pursuit of becoming a doctor was her "dream for the future" and it required a move to her dream school, UCLA, and the West Coast.

There are two factors that played a major role in her being selected for the Pan Am team at the age of 17 for the first Pan American Games to include fast pitch softball. First, she showed absolutely no sign of intimidation; the sense was that it was against her core belief as an athlete. Second, even though she had established herself as a shortstop, she was assigned to play second base at the trials, a position she had never played before, though you would never have guessed it. Dottie seemed as though she came into camp as a second baseman. She hustled, she was aggressive, and she played the new position flawlessly.

When I asked her about why she chose softball, I also got a strong dose of what she believes and how she learns, "Softball is a game for everyone. No matter what size, shape, race or ethnic background, the sport of softball has a place for you to experience and contribute. It teaches participants and spectators so many life lessons, such as how important each one of us is in the world and what a difference an individual can make toward the common goal or to the impact on society. Through the sport we learn that when we fall short of our goals we are not a failure because it is better to try and fail than to never try. We also learn that when we taste victory and feel we have succeeded that it doesn't mean we are better than someone else because true success is not based on the outcome of the game but instead is giving everything we have to be the best we can be in everything we do. That is all we can ask of ourselves – that is true success. Softball teaches us that it is not about 'I,' 'self,' but instead it is about working together with others to achieve the ultimate goal on the field: teamwork. Everyone is important, no matter what role they play on the team. The challenge of every athlete is to remove all doubt and dare to dream big, realizing that it takes hard work, dedication and commitment to bring those dreams into reality. Softball is more than a game, more than a sport – it is a learning platform for life."

When asked what she remembers about how softball and Dot came together, here's her memory: "I loved baseball, but was not allowed to play because girls were not permitted at that time in society to play organized sports. It seemed so unfair and at night while saying my prayers I asked God why he had given me so much talent with no opportunity to use it. I look back now and realized those were words of a child because I did not know what the future would hold. Then one day a Little League coach saw me throwing fastballs to my brother and asked me if I would play on his team. My prayers were about to be answered, but before I could reply he said, 'You will have to cut your hair really short and go by the name of Bob.' As much as I wanted to play, the price was way too high; I said; 'Sir, thank you but no thank you. If I have to hide who I am, I just don't feel right.' I walked over to a different field and started to play catch with a friend of mine when another coach came over to me and asked if I had a few minutes to talk to the head coach. When I met her, she asked me if I had ever heard of or played fast pitch softball. When I said 'No,' she replied, 'Well, it's just like baseball, but the ball is a little bigger, so get at third base and take a few ground balls.' Once I fielded those ground balls, I felt like I belonged. I knew it was right. When she asked how old I was and I said I was ten, and she looked shocked, I guess because the average age of the team was 22. So we had to go and ask my mom and dad. They both said that I could play on the team and the rest, I guess you could say, is history, since my softball career extended over thirty years."

Growing smarter for Dot became much more than a classroom or athletic field experience at UCLA. "From the university education to the athletic arena, my experience in college felt like we were a part of something special, a tradition of excellence not just as an athlete but more importantly as a person. It was more than studying and playing the sport, there always seemed to be a strengthening of an inner drive toward excelling in everything we do with the goal of making a difference in the lives of other people both on and off the field."

"While playing at UCLA we won the first NCAA Women's College World Series ever offered to our sport in 1982. Whether we won that championship or not, we knew we had been a part of something bigger than ourselves that would open the door of opportunity for others to pass through and hopefully in time expand on it. Today, you can see that expansion take place, as there are more women involved in NCAA sports. In the sport of fast pitch softball, there has been a growth in participation and talent parity, along with respect and prestige. It is fantastic that it is seen by millions of viewers on national television and that it grows in popularity. What makes it so great is that each viewer sees for themselves the amazing gifts each of these athletes possesses as well as the opportunity provided for them to express their talents at a high level of competition while receiving a great education.

"At UCLA, we enjoyed competing at the top collegiate level. We thrived on it because it always challenged us. The same is true playing at the national and international levels. It was great to watch, learn from, compete with and even meet elite athletes, whether they were my teammates or our competition. I have to admit, I find excitement in the opportunity to compete. What makes it so great is that you knew you were being challenged by some of the greatest of all time."

Prior to the start of the Olympic Games, when Dot was asked by reporters, "Aren't you nervous?" She responded, "Are you kidding? This is a celebration! I have been waiting for this my whole life."

"I have to admit that I never felt 'pressure.' Instead, the emotion I felt was always excitement. I could feel those butterflies spinning in my gut almost all the time before a game but they seemed to disappear once the game began. It was as though the 'movements' or 'feelings' inherent to the sport overcame any nerves or doubts. The game has begun. The intensity is on. It's showtime.

"This feeling of excitement on the field was always more of simply feeling 'alive' while practicing or playing the sport. It was genuine and real. It can be attributed to two major things. First, there was always a feeling of 'celebration' because I never took anything for granted. I always appreciated having the opportunity to play the game. Maybe it was because during my earlier years I was denied the opportunity and felt that frustration and confusion. Also, it was because I saw that my two older sisters were never given the chance. I learned to appreciate the chances and seize the moment. Second, but the number one reason why I feel the way I do on the field is; 'When I play, I feel God's pleasure. When we use the gifts that the Lord has given us we feel alive. We feel His presence and his blessings. We can rejoice and be glad. Everyone has been given gifts, which are meant to be experiences, enjoyed and shared. Let's live our lives as a celebration to the Lord. Trust in Him.'"

Grace Under Pressure

A number of the athletes in previous chapters have alluded to being in the moment and therefore not wasting their focus on pressure. Dr. Dot is the first one yet to use the word "celebration" to get to the heart of how she is able to get so much done without giving the impression of being in any way overwhelmed. Softball for her is simply a way for her God-given talents to enjoy expression – win or lose. However, she has learned, through a life of competing this way, that you don't lose very many games when you approach them with this attitude.

A rendition of Dr. Dot Richardson's career highlights can be found back on page 74, however, we thought it might be interesting to hear from her the moments that have stood out in her 30 years in softball. "My first ASA Women's Major National Championship (1975) was amazing and every one since. The first ever NCAA WCWS Championship, which we won and playing for the United States of America at all the World Championships; and Pan American Games. The 1981 ASA Women's Major National Championship in Houston, Texas, when we captured the first and only title for the Orlando Rebels organization. That championship game is still today considered one of the greatest comebacks in a final – we came from behind in the bottom of the 7th inning from a perfect game. And each National Championship won since then with the Raybestos Brakettes and California Commotion holds a special place in my heart. The opportunity to play at the highest level of competition at the 1996 & 2000 Olympic Games impacted each of us and the sport in historic ways. The ability to commentate for NBC at the 2004 Olympic Games in Athens, Greece was a blast. The earliest heightened memories in the sport for me reflect back to the '70s when I was playing for the Orlando Rebels. We always played in front of 1,000 fans or more. We were on the front page of the sports section with pictures and numerous articles about the games. Starting at 13 years of age playing at the Women's Major level, was extremely exciting and full of possibilities! Starting to play international ball, which began for me at seventeen years of age, brought a new level of excitement to the game by giving me the opportunity to represent our country through the sport I loved! Then came the opportunity to get a great education through college athletic scholarships. Awesome! All of it started to come together in a very unique and timely manner for my career."

And finally, in a 30-year career that involved the best players and coaches that softball had available, who were the people that had the most influence? "First and foremost influential people in my life are my parents. Mom and Dad believed in the gifts the Lord gave to me and let me play at the age of 10 with a women's team where the average age was 22, then at the age of 13 with a Women's Major Team. More importantly, Mom and Dad always showed their unconditional love and support for me to be who I am and do what I love to do. They taught me to appreciate God, enjoy the gift of life, treat others the way I would like to be treated and recognize the joy of serving others before oneself."

"On the field, the most influential people include a very long list but up at the top has to be the following: My coaches, including ASA Hall of Fame recipients Marge Ricker and Ralph Raymond, Sharron Backus, Kathy Veroni, and Kirk Walker. Coach Marge Ricker taught me professionalism, respect, dedication, focus, commitment to the sport and knowledge about the game. Coach Ralph Raymond demonstrated excellence and expertise along with honor and humility. Coach Sharron Backus taught me more about teamwork, striving for excellence, and tradition. Coach Kathy Veroni influenced me about how a coach can teach and inspire others to find more within them than they thought possible. Coach Kirk Walker is a symbol of commitment and dedication to help others achieve their dreams through the sport.

"There are so many athletes who have influenced me as a person and an athlete. Here are some of those: Snookie Mulder, Orlando Rebel center fielder and leadoff batter. When I was batgirl for that team she was the athlete I wanted to be as good as, so I set goals to one day break all of her records on the team. When I received the team program book, I had all the Rebels sign it. Snookie wrote simply: 'To Dot, the greatest batgirl.' It meant the world to me and taught me how much taking a little time to say or write a few words of recognition or encouragement to others can make an impact in their life. At a very young age, I watched, played with, or played against many legends: Joan Joyce, Sharron Backus, Irene Shea, Joyce Compton, Margie Wright, Willie Rose, Kathy Stillwell, Mary Lou Cushing, Snookie Mulder, Mickey Davis, Paula Noel, Diane Kalliam, Marilyn Rau and Donna Lopiano; in addition to other greats that my career just missed but was blessed to be able to meet, like Bertha Tickey, Carol Spanks, and Shirley Topley, to name a few.

"As I grew up, there were those great players that stood out, like Kathy Arendsen, Sue Enquist, Barbara Reinalda, Diane Schumacher, Suzy Brazney, Kathy Strahan, Michele Granger,

Michele Smith, Gina "Puppy" Vecchionie, Allison Rioux, Carol Hutchings, Julie Smith, Lori Stoll, Debbie Doom, Tracy Compton, Pam Newton, Suzie Gaw, Cindy Bristow, Rhonda Wheatley, Wendy Ward, Lisa Ishikawa, Pat Dufficy, LeAnn Jarvis, Lori Harrigan, Leah O'Brien-Amico, and Jennifer Brundage."

Dot informed us that her chapter "would not be complete without recognizing a couple extraordinary teammates that through the years are more than just standouts." They signify the "the Best of the Best." They represent all that is excellent in sport. They have shaped not only the game but also the history of our sport. They are the epitome of the ultimate softball player. Their qualities and character demonstrate intensity, commitment, determination, excellence, drive, confidence, passion, desire to impact something greater than self, sacrifice for team, knowledge of the game, willingness to learn, anticipation, "live in the moment" and a unique quality to "feel the game." She affectionately refer to these athletes as the "old breed" because they came into the sport at a different era, almost three decades later, than those pioneer legends that she observed as a young girl but they demonstrated their same spirit of intensity. Two of these three athletes are Laura Berg and Sheila (Cornell) Douty. In her mind, these two became the heart and soul of the sport because they always put in their whole heart and soul in every practice and game. They set an example for young players to follow. Laura, "Rookie," became the only American four-time Olympian in the sport. A graduate from Fresno State, WCWS National Champion, Women's Major National Champion, World Champion, Pan American Champion, and professional softball player. After retiring, she became a police officer and collegiate coach. She is always giving back to others. Sheila, "Ace of First Base," became a two time Olympic Gold Medalist. A graduate from UCLA, WCWS National Champion, Women's Major National Champion, numerous first team All-American selections, UCLA and

ASA Hall of Famer. She is a physical therapist and in her career opened doors for others to walk through. Dot says, "I am so proud to have played beside them on the practice and playing fields."

"The third of these three teammates is the most amazing and impactful athlete and teammate I have had the privilege to play with, and that is the one and only Lisa Fernandez. When time brought Lisa and me together as teammates with the Raybestos Brakettes and USA National teams, I saw firsthand the impact this one athlete had on the sport. Her talents and dominance as a pitcher, hitter, and fielder place her in a very unique category that very few athletes can reach. It became very obvious that Lisa would open doors of opportunity that our sport failed to provide in the past. The sport gained more and more recognition as Lisa dominated almost every category. As a senior at UCLA, she led the nation in batting average and lowest ERA as a pitcher, a feat that may never be duplicated. She seemed to be on every television talk show and news channel throughout the season. Her face was everywhere and the name 'Lisa Fernandez' became known in almost every household throughout the country. With the media outreach of UCLA and the exposure of the WCWS on ESPN, Lisa became a phenom and the sport benefited from it greatly. After her college career, Lisa continued to dominate and with USA Softball exposure, she began to open doors for softball players to be considered for individual corporate sponsorship opportunities. Lisa blazed a trail at all levels of the sport that many athletes are able to enjoy today. And through it all, Lisa never stopped being Lisa. Her commitment to the game is unparalleled and her desire to work to be the best that she can be at all times in unmatched. Lisa Fernandez; the best of the best."

"In mentioning all these impressive and impactful players of the game, you can see how their passion for softball evolved the sport into being much more than just a game. These Legends show that to be an athlete it requires and even demands their example of style, class, teamwork, drive towards perfection, and commitment to excellence. It also required the presence and importance of experience and knowledge; 'game smarts', and even the heightened awareness for anticipation of game skills and strategy. But I would say the most important influence these legends of the game demonstrated to me was the necessity to 'feel' the game and to always strive to live in the moment by becoming 'one with the ball.'"

Dr. Dot Richardson keeps churning the waters wherever she goes. And in her wake, something is better for having been near her. Thank you Dottie for being a solid source of inspiration for all these years.

Dr. Dot Richardson with one of her many fans, Kelly McGinnis

During her career at Texas A&M, Shawn Andaya compiled a pitching record of 114-28 for a winning percentage of .803. In 1987, she hurled the Aggies to the national title. (Photo courtesy Texas A&M Sports Information)

Chapter 9

Shawn Andaya
"The Pitcher Who Could"

Grace Under Pressure

When you are 5 feet 6 inches tall and weigh about 125 pounds, people might tend to look past you before a strenuous game. Those who made that mistake about Shawn Andaya soon learn to regret it. In that most tired of clichés – tired but true – what Shawn lacked in size, she made up in will, heart, and desire. When Shawn joined the back-to-back national championship (AIAW in 1982 and NCAA in 1983) Texas A&M Aggies, here's what she was thinking: "I think there was more pressure within my team than there was with me competing against somebody else or another school. I was walking on to a team full of All-Americans. And here I am: not a highly-recruited kid from California – because of my size I wasn't recruited very strongly. The pressure came from walking onto a national championship team. They can measure your body, but they can't measure your heart."

"Coach Brock had me warm up and pitch against the team. I think he wanted to see if the skinny girl who could pitch great to 18- year-olds could handle Division I collegiate players. The players lined up and I suddenly felt this adrenaline in my veins. I was small and most people underestimated me. I remember

Career Highlights
(Pitcher)

- Named to NCAA 25th Anniversary Team (2006)
- Three times named to WCWS All-Tournament Team 1984, 86, 87
- 2011 Elected to Texas Sports Hall of Fame. Is the first softball player elected to this Hall of Fame.
- Compiled 114-28 (.803) record during Texas A & M career
- Fanned 1,234 batters in 1,141.1 innings with 73 shutouts
- Compiled 0.43 ERA in college with 70 earned runs
- Member of NCAA College World Series Champion, 1987
- Member of NCAA College World Series runner-up, 1984, 86
- Hurled a perfect game in 1987 on championship day against UCLA, won 1-0
- Beat UCLA in championship game of 1987 WCWS, 4-1 drove in 2 runs
- Pitched longest game in WCWS history, 1984, 25 innings against Cal Poly Pomona. A & M won 1-0 with Andaya driving in the game's only run with a single
- Lost in national championship game of 1984 WCWS 1-0 to UCLA in 13 innings. She hurled 10.1, allowing five hits after replacing starter in third inning
- Senior year (1987) led NCAA in wins (36) and strikeouts (326)
- As a junior, hurled five no-hitters and pitched 44 consecutive scoreless innings
- As a freshman, shared NCAA lead in most wins (33)
- Assistant coach for Texas A & M for five years

thinking, 'I can do this. I am just as good as these girls.' I just went for it. Luckily, they kept me and Coach (Bob) Brock had another happy moment."

There was a similar "I can do it" moment that year against Oklahoma State University. "We were in Stillwater and our other pitcher, Yvette Lopez, started the game and got in a bit of trouble. The bases were loaded and the score was zero to zero. I had not warmed up and Coach Brock yelled to me on the bench, 'Shawn, let's go.' I was like, 'Okay.' I got out there, got my five warm-up pitches, and I was going to give it a shot.

"I don't know what it is about these situations, but the harder they are, the more I love them. The first batter strikes out, the second batter strikes out and the third batter strikes out. This was pretty huge. I felt that night that I was a real college player and that I could play with any of them. I was not afraid and I was actually excited to be put into that situation. I grew up that evening and I knew I could not just play at this level but excel."

We will skip to the 1984 WCWS because even though Shawn lost the championship games 1-0, 1-0 to UCLA and Debbie Doom, the 1984 games will always be remembered as the time when Shawn pitched more than 50 innings in the tournament (including an opening 25 inning 1-0 victory against Cal Poly Pomona) which carried over into a second day. Andaya always batted third for her team, and singled up the middle to drive in the only run of the game. By Shawn's account: "The [second baseman] actually stopped it, but she couldn't make a play on either myself or the girl going home. We were so desperate for a run and I think it was Josie Carter at third for us. I think as soon as I hit the ball she took off. The ball wasn't hit really hard but it made the second baseman go to the middle."

If you were watching the 2011 WCWS and got to see the Baylor-Missouri extra-inning game you would have heard the announcers describe the difficulty of pitching for so many days straight and finding yourself in an extra-inning game. But then again, you would hear them say, this is nothing like the feat performed by Shawn Andaya in 1984 – such is the respect shown for her grit and fortitude during that tournament. The game before the championship had Shawn on the topside of a 2-0 victory over UCLA and Debbie Doom, but her team couldn't scratch out a run and UCLA took home the trophy.

"She handled it really well," Brock commented after the crushing defeat where Trish Mang hit a home run off Shawn in the bottom of the 13th inning. Brock thought Shawn's experience with women's ASA ball had a lot to do with it. "When she handled the home run, one of the things I remember her saying was, 'Hey, we'll be back. In the next one we are going to take it.'" Brock continued, "I never saw Shawn really really upset. She said, 'We had a chance to do it, but we didn't pull it off…I'm a freshman and I've got some more time.'"

Here is Shawn's personal version of Grace Under Pressure: "When I think of Trish Mang's home run, ouch – that still hurts today. When you are a pitcher and you pitch, and you release the ball and nobody else touches it, and you lose on a walk-off home run in a national championship – I think it was probably the best learning experience I've ever had in my life. It was a motivator to come back and win it again, or be in that situation again."

"Because when you finish a game like that, you walk off and everybody says you did great. 'You should be so proud because you guys got second and you were in the national championship game.' To be honest with you, I know that's an honor and everything, but it feels just as bad as finishing 400th, because you had your eyes set on something and you were so close to getting it and one swing of the bat changed it that fast."

"I looked at it as a time to reflect. You can't make those types of mistakes in that type of game. I threw a flat rise ball to a big girl who was their No. 4 hitter. That was stupid. You cannot make those mistakes. You have to keep the ball down and in the ball park when those types of hitters come up."

So we fast-forward to 1987. Shawn Andaya is now the acknowledged leader of her Texas A&M Aggies and is taking them through the regionals into the WCWS for her final opportunity to win the big one. As always the team to beat was UCLA, and in their first WCWS meeting the Bruins send the Aggies into the loser's bracket. In Andaya's words: "I remember the national championship game. It was almost an out-of-body experience. We had gotten into the loser's bracket and I was looking at my team standing at the fence asking myself, 'Why was this so important to me? Here we are losing again against UCLA. This is my third time at this.' We came back the next morning. A lot of things have to happen to win a national championship. You need a lot of talent, but you have to have some luck along with it." That wasn't exactly what UCLA's Coach Backus was thinking on the other side of the field. All the luck the Aggies would need that day was in the look in Shawn Andaya's eyes. Backus watched as Shawn threw a perfect game to force an "if" game and in between games she remembers thinking that that kid wanted it more than anyone else that day. "You couldn't have driven her off the mound with a stick," the multiple Hall of Famer astutely noted. And that is one of the highest compliments Backus will give any player: "There goes a gamer."

Andaya threw 12 straight innings of perfect ball before giving up her first single. She won the first game 1-0, and batted in two in the nightcap in a 4-1 final. During the perfect game Andaya pulled a leg muscle running to first base. She talked Coach Brock out of not hitting in the second game, "I had been hitting all year. Please let me hit." In the 48 innings that Texas A & M played in the WCWS that year, Andaya pitched all 48, giving up only one earned run. Her ERA was 0.15.

Growing Smarter

Shawn's father Robert had pitched fast pitch in the men's Open division in California. He would often go out to the garage and pitch to Shawn's mother. After a year or so of watching her Dad pitch, one day her mom missed the ball. Shawn ran, picked up the ball and threw it back to Dad. "I pitched it back to him and it was a perfect strike," said Shawn, "My Dad said, 'Wow, that was pretty good. Can you do that again?'" She could.

Although Shawn had not been given any instruction, she said, "While I was sitting there and watching him for so long, I picked up the mechanics of pitching. So from that day forward, I had instant success even in the backyard. I adored and loved softball. Practice was never to be a problem. I loved practicing as much as playing. That's when you really love the sport."

She did have to adjust when pitching to her first batters. "I could pitch fast but I kept looking at the batter's face, and what I looked at, that's what I hit. I learned that day that I was accurate and that I needed to focus on the catcher's glove and not the batter's head" Her father had a strategy for helping her develop: she played with older women rather than staying in her age group. It gave her maturity beyond her years. It was only during her last year in high school that she focused on 18-under play. However, her all-around play was good enough for her to be named the California Player of the Year for Lodi High School.

According to Coach Brock, "I have to give her credit for working hard and everything, but I've got to give that Dad a lot of credit too. When she was growing up, he taught her a lot. One of the things he worked on a lot was the attitude toward the game. Her father did a good job. Her parents were very thankful she came to A&M. He brought her here. I am so excited that she came here. 'She's yours,' he said, and never said another word except to cheer her on."

Brock said that the good relationship Shawn had with her father was one of the reasons she could excel in college. "She could always talk to him in a reasonable manner, which is different from some of today's parents and how they treat their children. Parents today would overreact to their kids' abilities, putting unrealistic demands on children."

Doing Good by Being Good

As Shawn got used to the idea that she was a player who was there to stay, she increasingly took on a leadership role in her program. Here is how Bob Brock described it: "She was just a leader all the time. She never really let things go to her head. She was always humble and always looked out after the other person, like someone who struck out with the bases loaded. She was always there for somebody. 'I'll pick you up, let's get that run. I'll do my part, you gotta do your part.' She always seemed to be pulling for the underdog, like the person batting ninth. She might carry the catcher's bag one day. She could be counted on to be first in everything. She was just a constant leader.

"I think she knew pretty much within herself that when she walked out to the mound she had a chance to win. She never, never showed any cockiness. If you didn't see her pitch, you wouldn't think she was any different than any other player on that team. She always looked like a regular person. Once you went out and saw her pitch you wouldn't know she was the ace of the staff. She knew she could pitch. She didn't have to be told all day. It didn't bother her if someone said, 'Shawn, we didn't get you the runs.' She would say, 'But I gave up the hit.'"

Brock has had Shawn talk to his Sam Houston State players. "You can walk in there and you can tell that this girl has been a winner," said Brock, "She's got that air about her. My family loves her; my kids grew up with her. It would be great to go back in time and have a chance to coach Shawn for one more inning."

When Shawn Andaya pitched, Brock didn't worry. "She never said she couldn't pitch a game," said Brock, "'Shawn, you're on today. So I'm going to get my lawn chair and drink a glass of tea today.' She would look at me and smile."

After her college career Shawn tried data management, but within four years was back with the Aggies as an assistant coach under Coach Brock. When Brock moved to Sam Houston University Andaya decided it was time for her to make a career change and has devoted herself to non-profit causes ever since.

Her first non-profit was at the Boys and Girls Club of the Brazos Valley. It gave her a chance to work directly with boys and girls in the community. She stayed five years as Vice President of Marketing and Resource Development. She then took a job as Executive Director of the Children's Museum of the Brazos Valley. Here she was able to use her combined leadership experience to "build a team of employees and work within the community to build a team of financial supporters." She spent 7 years there.

In 2010, Shawn Andaya moved on to working at non-profit hospitals. "I moved on to Scott and White Hospital as a gift officer raising money for hospital projects and children's programs." She is currently employed by the St. Joseph Foundation as Director of Major Gifts. She raises money for a six county region and says that she plans to be here for a while. Good luck to you and those counting on you – they couldn't have made a better choice.

Shawn is married to former Texas A&M basketball player, Al Pulliam. Shawn and Al have two children, AJ (17) and Trey (13). Al and Shawn have been married for 18 years.

Shawn Andaya consistently batted third in the Texas A&M lineup and in the 1987 NCAA WCSW championship game against UCLA she drove in two of her team's four runs. (Photo courtesy of Texas A&M Sports Information Department)

Debbie Doom compiled a 13-4 record in the Women's College World Series in pitching UCLA to three national titles. (Photo courtesy of Debbie Doom)

Chapter 10

DEBBIE DOOM
"WINNING THE BIG ONES"

Grace Under Pressure

Since 1982, there have been hundreds of pitchers who have appeared in the Women's College World Series (WCWS). Do you know the only player to win three WCWS Final games for her team? Look to the left and you will see Debbie Doom as she was in 1982, 1984 and 1985. A 1983 appearance in the Finals is notably missing. Since I heard the story behind this independently from Debbie, Dot Richardson, and Coach Sharron Backus, I will report their observations. After the meal before the start of the tournament, a number of the UCLA Bruins came down with stomach ailments that had them feeling sick and even throwing up throughout the next days. Even with these problems, the Bruins came in third that year. Therefore, you can't fault the members of the teams for feeling bad that they lost their chance to win the WCWS a fourth time in a row.

There is something else a bit strange about Debbie Doom finding herself in the pitcher's circle for the final game of the three tournaments. Sharron Backus was a firm believer in Ralph Raymond's approach to pitching rotations: 1) find two or more

Career Highlights
(Pitcher)

- Named to NCAA 25th Anniversary Team leading UCLA to 3 titles
- Four-time All-American, compiled a 73-16 record (.820)
- Had 0.29 career ERA at UCLA and struck out 954
- NCAA strikeout champion in 1982 (freshman) and 1983
- Hurled 56 shutouts, seven no-hitters and eight one-hitters
- Compiled a 13-4 record in WCWS play, 0.57 ERA, 176 strikeouts in 146 innings
- 1984 won The Honda Award- nation's best college softball player
- Named WCWS All-Tournament Team three times (1982, 84, 85)
- Named ASA All-American eight times: 1980, 81, 82, 86, 87, 89, 91, 92
- Member of ASA national champion 1979 and 1987
- Named Most Valuable Player – 1980 ASA national championship
- Member of 1982 USA National team (represented by Orlando Rebels) that finished fourth in ISF World Championship. Compiled 3-1 record with 36 strikeouts in 21 innings.
- Member of 1990 USA National Team that won the gold medal
- Compiled 4-1 record in ISF World Championship play with 48 strikeouts in 26 innings and an ERA of 0.27)
- Member of the pro champion Orlando Wahoos, 1997-98
- 1997 compiled 15-2 record with 0.42 ERA
- 1998 compiled 9-1 record with 0.84 ERA
- 1997 named MVP of the championship series, 3-0 record

pitchers who were relatively equal in talent and capacity to win; 2) use them alternatively with no regard for opponent. (e.g., if Debbie pitched Monday it was Tracy Compton's turn to pitch Tuesday). According to Debbie, Sharron was the kind of coach with a very slow hook. "She told us when we went out there, 'It's your game to win or lose – don't look to the dugout to bail you out when you get in a jam.'"

"Well, two of those years Tracy Compton was due to pitch but she got hurt or was sick. She couldn't physically go," said Backus, "and the year she could go was '83 and the team was sick. So really she was a victim of circumstances as far as what befell her during that period. She had a great year, ready to go into it, then something would happen. Tracy was going to pitch in all of them (1982, 1983, 1984, 1985) I did a lot like the Brakettes did with the rotation of Donna (Lopiano), and Joan (Joyce), Donna, Joan. That type of thing, but with Tracy sick or hurt she couldn't go. I mean, the poor kid was snake-bit her whole college career. She had great conferences and non- conference games during the season, but when it came to playoffs, she just couldn't answer."

When asked about what made Doom a difference maker, Backus said, "Her size, number one. She was one of the few pitchers over six feet tall and when she took that stride off the mound she was out of the circle. She was so illusory. She mesmerized the hitters because she had about eight different speeds and her ball moved. We were very lucky to get her. Debbie stepped up, she had very good seasons, but when it came to the big game she was very focused and very meticulous with her preparation and execution."

In 1980, before UCLA and when she was still a teenager, Debbie Doom put on a show at the ASA Nationals that alerted the establishment there was a new pitcher to be reckoned with. She was playing for the Sun City Saints and after her team lost its first game and was put into the loser's bracket, she was handed the ball and kept it the rest of the way. In the course of striking out 70 batters in 58 innings and winning 6 in a row before getting the second loss which left the team in third place, she established her signature deliberate, slow-paced delivery. Then, in a flash, the ball was on top of the batter at nearly 70 miles per hour. Even then she had the two crucial directions – up and down – and could throw with control as slow as she wanted. No wonder she was sought-after.

One thing that may not be known is that Sue Enquist, who was playing in the ASA National Championship for the Raybestos Brakettes and who had a connection to Sharron Backus, called Sharron and told her to sign this kid, based entirely on what Sue had seen. Debbie describes a very pleasant recruiting trip to UCLA and feeling very comfortable with the team's commitment to excellence.

If you would like another example of how flexible Debbie was and determined she was to win under all circumstances, you could go to the 1985 NCAA WCWS, where UCLA came out of the loser's bracket to face Texas A&M, whose ace, Shawn Andaya, had sent them into the bracket by a score of 2-0. Championship day was played on one day then, with the if-necessary game following the championship game. In 1985, Debbie Doom pitched 20 straight innings of shutout ball to beat A&M, and Andaya, 1-0.

Just one other experience for good measure: in the 1991 Pan Am Games, Debbie pitched back-to-back perfect games, striking out about 17 in each game, according to her recollection.

Growing Smarter

Debbie Doom began sports as a bowler, like her mother, and started to take bowling lessons when she was about eight or nine. It was her father's decision to have her quit bowling and start pitching softball. In those days she didn't have the sense that she had much say in the decision. According to Debbie, "Well, I was always a pitcher when I played softball. But I can't say that I was really a Pitcher. I didn't know how to do it, of course. I pretty much did it like I bowled. It wasn't until I was 13 that my dad got me a coach. I was living in Tempe, Arizona and one of the coaches there, Hank Duffy, became my pitching coach. He was the one who gave me my basic mechanics. Duffy was really into mechanics and that fit very well with my dad (David) and me. We have analytic minds. We like to know how things fit together so you get the most out of it. I guess I got that (trait) from Dad."

Duffy worked with Doom to show her how to use her height (6 feet 2 inches) to her advantage, extending her stride and disguising her pitches by letting go of the ball at the calf level instead of at her hip. Doom found she had a natural downspin, giving her a drop that fell six inches. She later added a rise and a changeup.

During Doom's time with the Sun City Arizona Saints, she was extremely fortunate to have as her battery mate during her 6-1 loser's bracket run ASA Hall of Famer Marilyn Rau. The catcher batted .520 to lead the tourney in hitting and was a steadying hand for the 17–year-old in her first national tournament. For her ASA effort, Debbie Doom was voted tournament MVP. Here is her reaction: "It was very exciting, but I was a really quiet, withdrawn kid. The attention was a little hard to deal with. But when I was out there pitching, that was the easy part. I always felt comfortable out there. Didn't matter who was watching or how many people were watching when I was in the circle. It didn't matter. I was just focused on what I was doing."

The value of growing smarter came into play for Debbie in her decision to select UCLA. "UCLA," Debbie said, "put academics ahead of the sport. They wanted to make sure they were getting people who were able to keep a good enough GPA to be eligible to play and also to graduate. They wanted good students who were going to graduate. When I was there – all four years that I was there – we were the top team at UCLA for GPA. We had a good team and a lot of smart girls."

Doom was named All-American four times and to the WCWS All-Tournament team three times (1982, 1984, 1985). Before it was broken in 2006 by Alicia Hollowell of Arizona, Debbie Doom held the record for total strikeouts in a WCWS with 62. Doom finished her career with 952 strikeouts and a 73-16 (.820 winning percentage) record for a 0.29 ERA, allowing 30 earned runs in 725.2 innings. She led the NCAA pitchers in strikeout ratio in 1982 (10.1) and 1983 (8.8).

In recognition of her accomplishments, Doom was named to the NCAA All Decade team in 1991, and the 25th Anniversary NCAA Division I Women's Softball All-Star Team in 2006. She was inducted into the UCLA Athletic Hall of Fame in 1995.

Reflecting on her college career, Debbie said: "I will tell you how Sharron told it to us. I love the atmosphere at UCLA. We were told we were winners from the start. You need to live up to being winners. What Sharron always told Tracy and me was, 'That's your game. If you mess it up, you are going to have to stay in there and get out of it.' So I took that to heart. Every game I pitched I was going to do my best that we could win."

"You have to make sure you are in good shape to be able to last through those extra-inning games, and it takes a lot of mental preparation. That was the kind of thing that I had learned playing on the Saints which was reinforced throughout college and then on the International teams."

Doing Good by Being Good

In 1985, Debbie was playing for the American team in Sydney, Australia when a moment of particular team support and compassion occurred that has stuck with her to this day. Again, it's nice to hear it from the perspective of the athlete: "I had been an All-American and made the team coached by Carol Spanks and Margie Wright. Obviously we had an awesome team, all the best players. I always learned a lot from the people around me. I am more of an observer. But I will tell you what happened there that was pretty special!

"There was this one game. It always seemed that it was always me [pitching] when the clouds came. I was the rain pitcher. If it was going to rain I was going to pitch. It had just poured in Sydney, Australia, where we were. There was so much water on the field, it was above my cleats. For some reason they decided to go ahead and play the game. We were playing against China. They were very tough. So I got the call to pitch that game. I did my warm up.

"Of course the hardest thing about playing in pouring rain is there is nothing dry you can wipe your hands off. You start with the socks but after a while they are soaked. So I did my best to keep my hand dry. Everybody on the team was trying to help. I could see the people on the bench. They would get the balls, wipe them down and make sure of good aim tossing them to the umpires. Everybody was doing their part. Total team effort for sure. I don't know how they did it.

"It was hard to hold that ball. I tried to let nothing bother me, whether it was rain or field conditions. Stayed focused on my catcher. Did the best I could. I ended up striking out a lot. Carol Spanks told me it was one of her most memorable games."

Debbie Doom has been in a career's worth of memorable games and she has left a mark as wide as her legendary stride. For all of us who have witnessed the deliberate and methodical way she got the job done, time after time, we salute a woman who could play and win under all conditions.

Part 2

*Experts,
Authorities,
Coaches & Players*

USA Head Coach Mike Candrea confers with Tairia Flowers, a member of the 2008 USA National Team. (Photo by USA Softball)

Chapter 11

MIKE CANDREA
"SOFTBALL'S JOHN WOODEN"

Grace Under Pressure

O r perhaps, John Wooden, the late UCLA basket-ball coach famous for winning 10 NCAA basket-ball championships with players like Kareem Abdul Jabbar and Bill Walton is basketball's Mike Candrea. In the period between 1991 and 2010, Candrea's University of Arizona Wildcats have either won first place in the NCAA WCWS (8 times: 1991, 1993, 1994, 1996, 1997, 2001, 2006, 2007) or come in second (5 times: 1992, 1995, 1998, 2002, 2010). Their second-place finish in 1995 was to UCLA, which was forced to vacate the WCWS title because of recruiting inconsistencies.

In 2004 Mike was named head coach of the USA Olympic Team, an honor that he also held in 2008. The 2004 team had a 9-0 record on the way to a third USA Gold Medal, beating the other tournament teams by a combined score of 51-1. The 2008 team was 8-0 before reaching the gold medal game where it lost 3-1 to Japan.

Career Highlights
(Coach)

- 2004, Head Coach USA Olympic Team – won gold medal
- 2008, Head Coach USA Olympic team – won silver medal
- Named Head Coach of the NCAA 25th Anniversary Softball Team
- 2003, Coached USA National team to gold medal in first World Cup and ISF World Championship
- 2007, Coached USA National team to gold medals in Canada Cup, World Cup, Pan American Games and Japan Cup
- Coached the University of Arizona to eight NCAA titles and five runners-up
- Has compiled a record of 1272 wins, 277 losses and 2 ties at Arizona (.821 winning percentage) 1986-2011
- Coached Arizona to eight NCAA national titles: 1991, 1993, 1994, 1996, 1997, 2001, 2006, 2007
- Four time NFCA Division I Coach of the year
- Nine Pac 10 conference regular season titles
- Named Pac-10 Coach of the Year 10 times
- 1984 and 1985 coached Central Arizona College to junior college national titles
- 1984-85 Named NJCAA Coach of the year.
- Coached at Central Arizona College from 1981-1985, complied 185-69 Record (.728 Winning percentage)
- Member of the NFCA Hall of Fame
- Bachelor's degree and master's degree from ASU

Since his time at Central Arizona College and continuing through his tenure at the University of Arizona, one characteristic stands out above all: he loves softball and can dedicate himself to the game tirelessly. You might be surprised, however, to learn that he has never played in a fast pitch game. In fact, given his original preferences, he would have happily continued to take the path of being a teacher and baseball coach.

Candrea played baseball at Central Arizona College until an injury his sophomore year ended his playing career. "I knew I was going into coaching and teaching. I didn't realize I would get an opportunity at the college level immediately. But it so happened that I got asked to be an assistant coach at Central Arizona College for the baseball program. That was kind of interesting because that year (1976) we won the national championship and I'm thinking to myself, 'You know, this is fun, it's fun, it's not that tough. And little do you know when you are that young that it gets a little tougher every year.'"

Although Candrea never dreamed of going into softball, Central Arizona Athletic Director George Young, a four-time Olympian in track and field, had other plans. Here is Mike Candrea's memory of their career-changing conversation: "Young said to me, 'Mike, I need your help. Would you consider taking over the women's softball program for a year?' I looked at him like, 'What did I do wrong, George? I'm a pretty good baseball coach.' He explained, 'We are getting more funding for women's athletics right now and we need to ramp this up a little bit.'"

Young said it would give Candrea a chance to see what he could do on his own." "And that was the beginning of it," said Candrea, "I said I would do it for a year, but I really wanted to coach baseball." Those who coach women's softball often find they really enjoy it even if they weren't expecting to. "After the first year, I kind of fell in love with it," said Candrea, "I go watch the nationals. I am thinking, God, we can win this thing. I just need a couple of players. So I end up getting Connie Clark. Back then they were almost kind of overlooking her. I thought she was a phenom. We won national [junior college] championships back-to-back in 1984-85. And I was getting a bit tired of egos in baseball. You know every kid thinks he is going to be in the Big Leagues. They really didn't do a great job in the classroom because they all thought they weren't going to need it.

"And it was kind of refreshing to coach the emotions of the female athlete. I felt that it was easier to turn the emotions into positives without being concerned about egos. The greatest thing I thought was the female athlete had no bad habits to break. They hadn't had the repetition that the guys have had by the time they were in college. They were easier to change and fix – that has changed a little bit today. But you know I think that was what it was that really kind of caught my attention and caught my interest. And the rest is history."

This part of the story is under the heading of Grace Under Pressure because it once again identifies how the best of the best can turn the mundane, daily processes of doing their job into a celebration of the game they love. These are people who do not associate playing softball with struggle, unless something unforeseen and terrible crosses their path. For Mike Candrea and the 2004 Olympic softball team, that event struck suddenly in the form of an aneurism that took the life of Candrea's wife, Sue, just a few weeks before the start of the Athens Olympics.

College wives come in two primary types: they are either not seen very much at all, or they become wrapped up in the family atmosphere that is at the heart of a supportive group-focused team. I met Sue and knew her to be the latter kind of coach's spouse. She was fond of people and they liked her in return. Her loss was not just to the coach and his family, but to the extended team family as well.

In retrospect it should not have been a surprise, but Mike

divided his world into two parts. Whatever he was feeling privately about his loss would have to wait until after the Olympics responsibilities had been dispatched to be fully expressed. In the meantime, the outside world would see a man and his team mourning the loss of an intimate relative who would surely want them to keep their eyes on the prize. Elizabeth Merrill on ESPN.com has written a very touching article (He Grieved his Wife's Death, Now U.S. Softball Coach Must Carry On) about that time of loss and the conditions associated with it. She also puts into perspective positive changes that have occurred in Coach Candrea's personal life as well as his reflections. It is an excellent example of how we must sometimes adapt to horrendous conditions coming at the worst possible time with as much grace as we can muster. When teams are sufficiently fortunate to establish the support system of a healthy family, even intolerable grief can find a way to become tolerable, as well as a lesson in grace under pressure. Mike's general demeanor has a stoic quality on the field. It is often difficult to determine whether he has just won or lost a national championship if you see him a couple of hours after a game. He took that quality with him to Athens and showed the team how to grieve with dignity without using the grief as an excuse for poor play.

Growing Smarter

If you were a career baseball player and coach who has just been told by your boss that he has plans for you on a softball field, what is the first thing you would do? Remember, unlike most other coaches at that time, you didn't have the advantage of even playing fast pitch softball. Mike Candrea decided to watch men's fast pitch games to get a sense of how the process of winning occurs. "I have always been a process-oriented individual," said Candrea, "So the one thing I have always been able to do, even when I was playing, was to always embrace the process. I always loved the process of getting better every day."

Early on, he noticed that the men's game hinged around speed and power. Add strong pitching and defense and you have the pillars of a powerful winning strategy. Candrea, because of his experience with nine-inning baseball games, was acutely aware of the shorter seven-inning complete softball game and the heightened need to use speed and power to get a lead as early in the game as possible. Once your team is in front, let the other team feel the pressure while your team neutralizes pressure from the other direction with strong pitching and defense.

The teacher in Candrea understands the broad sweep of the game but revels in its nuances, calling them "the little building blocks that have to take place to be able to perform at the right time and at a high level."

"Every day I get up in the morning and look forward to going to work. I always tell people that I've never worked a day in my life because I have been able to do something I have a passion for and that I love. I look back and I have been on a baseball or softball field since I was five years old. So it's a pretty unique life to have that opportunity."

The process perspective brings with it an appreciation for what it takes to continue to hone one's craft over many years of top level play. "One thing I always tell people. When I coached the Olympic team the one great thing that I took from it is that I got to see some of our good players play the game at 27, 28, 29, 30 years old where they had game maturity."

He went on, "When you get a chance to see someone like Lisa (Fernandez) and watch her prepare and watch her control her mindset during a game, it's pretty phenomenal to watch...I remember a time during the Pan American Games when we were in the Dominican Republic. Every time we went to a Pan Am Games the balls never got there. You think that you are going to throw a yellow ball with red seams. I remember getting there and the balls got lost. So they hand us a white ball with white seams.

"Well, luckily, Lisa was starting that game. I remember Cat and the younger girls were standing around when I handed Lisa the ball. And she goes, 'I love this ball.' Instead of saying, 'What is this?' the mindset was 'I love this ball.' And no one said a word about the ball from then on. But that was the kind of player Lisa was. She has a different mindset than most."

"Fernandez prepared herself every game mentally and was consistent every year. Amazing thing, she excelled and did it year after year. Once she got to the top level she stayed there and always had a little different wrinkle every year. She was smart enough to know how to stay a little bit ahead of the curve."

Another player who is closely associated with Candrea is Jennie Finch, who had 60 consecutive wins between her sophomore and senior years, culminating in a national championship during her perfect 32-0 junior year. Jennie also played on both the 2004 and 2008 Olympic teams. According to Mike, the two had a rapport based on understanding what it took to keep a balance in one's personal, professional and faith-based parts of their lives. But the 60-game streak was just part of the game, as Mike quotes in the 2004 Olympic Players' Guide: "Yesterday is history, tomorrow is a mystery, today is a gift and that's why we call it the present."

Doing Good by Being Good

With an overall coaching record of 1,361 wins, 314 losses and 2 ties for an .812 winning percentage, a University of Arizona team record of seventeen seasons with 50 wins or more (with five seasons 60 or more wins), as well as International USA victories in the Pan Am Games in 2003; World Cup and ISF World Championship in 2006; and Canada Cup, World Cup,

Pan American Games and Japan Cup in 2007, Mike Candrea has surely earned his reputation as a best of the best teacher, coach and statesman in the world of fast pitch softball.

Conversations about the Olympics bring Mike to thoughts about the continued growth of his sport. "I think the college game is well-connected, and I think it's in good hands right now because people have an interest in the WCWS and games played throughout the year, and the NCAA is smart enough to know that this is a sport that can draw people. I mean, whoever thought that we would play a mid-week game against Creighton last night and draw 2,850, almost 3,000? We were just about sold out."

Candrea is also seeing some competitive trends in high school aged players that he believes are changing their mindset away from what is required to be compete successfully at the college level. When asked about the emphasis of getting scholarship commitments earlier in a high school player's career, Mike had these cautionary thoughts: "I think [mindsets] have changed even more so now with early commitments that kids are making. A kid makes an early commitment to a school when she is a sophomore in high school. She starts wearing the colors and is very excited. She kind of gets to live the dream for two or three years while still in high school. Then, all of a sudden, she gets here, the game starts and reality sets in. She's thinking, 'Now, I have to go out there and perform.' There is a bit of a learning curve."

Mike's strong suggestion is that even when a sophomore makes a commitment to a school, she continues to work and improve. It is too easy to think that the scholarship is the carrot and all that has to happen is to put your game on cruise control until you get to the next level. That plan becomes a recipe for recruiting mistakes, an unhappy student athlete and a wasted scholarship for the program

He is also somewhat leery about a change at the high school

summer ball level, which he says has moved away from playing games under real competitive conditions, to playing for exposure to college recruiters. "Kids today really don't care if they win, lose, or draw as long as they played well and they showed well," said Candrea. "I think that's what has affected the competitiveness of this generation."

As he sees the game change he notices fewer opportunities to gain experience under the pressure of win-lose events. It is that experience that he feels galvanizes a player like Lisa Fernandez to adapt and expand her capabilities. Without that experience, girls are prone to make the same mistakes as boys: too many repetitions of mistakes and too many game conditions that are designed to feel like pressure-free opportunities to show individual skills.

When Mike Candrea looks out onto a softball or baseball field, the teacher in him wants to notice physical and mental maturity being developed on the field and the lover of the game is ready to enjoy moments of tension with the resulting opportunities for growing smarter or demonstrating grace under pressure. When that is absent, you might as well be judging talent by how far a ball goes out of the park during batting practice.

When asked to reflect on personal highlights of his career, these are Mike's thoughts: "I always tell people that every NCAA championship that I've been a part of has been a great chapter in my life, but when you're given the opportunity to coach the Olympic team you wear the red, white and blue and it's pretty special…the national anthem today is a completely different song than it was before my experience with the Olympic team. Any time you can hear that in a foreign country, it's pretty emotional. It brings me back to that time…I was very grateful and very fortunate to have the opportunity."

Ralph Raymond was the first coach of the USA National Team when softball made its debut in the Olympics in 1996. Raymond also coached the 2000 USA National Team to a gold medal in the Olympics.
(Photo by USA Softball)

Chapter 12

RALPH RAYMOND
"DEAN OF WOMEN'S SOFTBALL"

Grace Under Pressure

Ask anyone at the top echelon of softball leadership and you will be told that Ralph Raymond is a coach who believes in keeping the game simple and free of gimmicks. Look at his composite record and you will see that he has left a string of championships and gold medal performances wherever his teams have been. For starters we can look at the Raybestos Brakettes, an ASA women's Major team that he coached between 1966 and 1994. During that 29-year period, his team won 19 ASA National Championships and were runners up eight times, which means that his teams were in the championship game 27 out of 29 years.

He coached the USA National team to gold medals in three Pan Am Games (1979, 1995, 1999), five ISF World Championships (1974, 1978, 1986, 1990, and 1994 with a 52-0 record); and assorted other international gold medal prizes that can be found among his career highlights on page 120. But most im-

Career Highlights
(Coach)

- *Coached USA National Team to gold medals in 1996 and 2000 Olympic Games*
- *Coached Raybestos Brakettes to 19 ASA National Championships 1966-1994 and eight runners-up*
- *Compiled record of 1,991 wins and 162 losses (.925 winning percentage)*
- *Coached USA National Teams to:*
    Five ISF World Championships: 1974, 1978, 1986, 1990, and 1994 (52-0 record)
- *Gold medal in 1992 World Challenger Cup.*
- *Gold medal in 1993 Intercontinental Cup*
- *Gold medals in World Games One and World Games Two*
- *Gold medal in 1994 South Pacific Classic*
- *Gold medal in 1995 Superball*
- *Gold medals in three Pan American Games (1979, 95, & 99)*
- *Silver medal in 1983 Pan American Games*
- *Member of the ISF Hall of Fame, ASA National Softball Hall of Fame, Connecticut ASA Hall of Fame, Massachusetts ASA Hall of Fame*
- *1950 graduate of the University of Miami, Fl., where he played basketball and football for one year and baseball for four years.*
- *In 2011, at age 87, coached the Worcester Hawks in the ASA GOLD National Championship*

portantly, when the USA entered its first Olympic Games in 1996 followed by its second in 2000, Ralph was named head coach of the gold medal teams.

He is a member of the ISF Hall of Fame, the ASA National Softball Hall of Fame, the Connecticut ASA Hall of Fame and the Massachusetts ASA Hall of Fame. He has been a friend ever since I met him more than 35 years ago and a thorough gentleman on and off the field. It could be safely said during his 29 year tenure with the Brakettes that all roads to the ASA National Championships led through Stratford, Connecticut, where Raybestos played its home games.

Mike Candrea, who coached under him for one of the non-Olympic USA teams in the early '90s, remembers him as a solid coach whom he enjoyed going to mass with on Sundays. Dot Richardson, in her book *Living the Dream*, had this to say about Ralph in her chapter on Role Models: "Ralph is one of the best motivators I've ever been around. He's a strong Christian, a strong family man and he's one of the strongest coaches I've ever had. I say that because he believes in his players so much that they automatically believe in themselves. He expects only your best and he knows that's what he's going to get. No more, no less.

"He is the winningest coach in the history of modern sports. I didn't know that until I read it in a magazine. He's won more games, by percentage, than any other coach in any other sport...Basically, his success stems from his ability to attract quality players. He reaches for those who strive to perform at their highest level and they deliver for him. He has had fantastic talent play for him, and he knows how to keep people with talent happy. That's not easy all the time. He did it without writing goals on a chalkboard. He surrounded himself with people who shared his inner drive.

"More important, with Ralph, you knew you were part of a family. He taught me how to lead without being a dictator. He did it through presence. You respected him so much that you wanted to please him…

"Maybe because he's a man coaching a women's team, he never treated us the way a lot of coaches do. He never got involved in our personal lives unless we went to him with a problem. He kept it strictly business, which meant we all knew there were no excuses with Ralph. He didn't play someone because he didn't want them to be upset. He gave everyone a shot during the season, then in big games and national championship he went with the players he felt were the best.

"Ralph taught me that there would be teammates, whom you don't get along with or whom you didn't really care about off the field, but when you step on the field you respect each other. He never had low expectations because we were women. Sometimes that happens with coaches who are afraid to set high goals with their players because they think, 'Oh, they're girls. I have to handle them with kid gloves.' Not Ralph. And that was his best quality. He respected our talents as athletes." (pp. 155-6)

Because Ralph Raymond did not believe in over-coaching, he allowed Olympic rookie Stacey Nuveman to call her own game behind the plate in the 2000 Games, even though her battery mates had many more years of experience. If you're not ready to be in the line of fire, you had better not show up. Stacey remembers how it felt to feel trepidation in the midst of his confidence. The result was another gold medal with the team coming back strong after three losses.

Growing Smarter

Ralph Raymond seems born to be a teacher and coach, but after graduating from the University of Miami in 1950 with four years of baseball and one each of basketball and football he went to work for the Wyman-Gordon Company from 1950 to 1968.

While there he coached American Legion baseball, high school football and a couple of men's fast pitch softball teams. In 1961 he went down to Cochituate, Massachusetts to meet with the sponsor of a women's team. "When I left for the meeting I wasn't sure I wanted to do that. I was more interested in baseball, but I went to Cochituate and stayed there 4 years."

Known as a coach who won the big games, Raymond's team was invited to participate in the annual July tournament in Stratford, Connecticut, the Brakettes' hometown. "So we went down there and beat [the Brakettes]," Raymond said. The tournament organizers figured the Brakettes would win and even had their names engraved on the first place plaques. "We had to wait until midnight to get the plaques changed to read Cochituate Motors," said Raymond.

The win proved to be a stepping stone of Raymond's career. The late Bill Simpson, then Chairman of the Board and President of Raybestos, phoned Raymond a day after the tournament ended and asked him to join the Raybestos coaching staff, which included Vincent (Wee) Devitt, who was the first manager of Raybestos' men's team, the Cardinals, from 1948-51.

On paper Devitt was listed as the manager, but in reality Raymond did the real work. "The thing that a lot of people don't understand – and I've never said it – is that Wee Devitt let me run the team from the day I got there," Raymond said. "I called the plays. I ran the practices. Wee handled the money end of it, the travel end of it. That type of thing." In his first two years, 1966-1967, Raymond won the ASA national title with records of 74-4 and 67-2 before officially taking over for good in 1968. From 1971-1978 the team won eight consecutive ASA Major national titles.

Throughout his career Raymond hated to lose, and didn't change his philosophy even as the athletes changed. "I hated to lose. When we lose a ball game I want a legitimate loss. If we lose it because of mental mistakes, I get upset and I think about it. But if we lose it legitimately – where the other team beats you on the field, between the lines – that's okay." Ralph Raymond believes in five principles for putting together a winning team. The first of these is pitching; the second is defense, because if you have a sound defense a ball club should be in every game; the third is speed; the fourth is savvy (understanding the game and attitude); and the fifth is hitting.

Raymond's record made him the logical choice to be the USA's first Olympic coach. "Being named softball's first Olympic coach was the pinnacle point in my career. Winning the gold medal meant that I'd finally reached the top of the mountain," said Raymond. In 1996, Raymond wasn't involved in selecting the players on the team. If you go back to Dot Richardson's words about coach Raymond you can see that he had a very clear picture of how he wanted to use the talent available to him, particularly in championship situations. "They had a selection committee and I wasn't involved in picking players. As far as I was concerned, in 1996 I had to take what they gave me. Some of the people I got I really couldn't use. In 2000, instead of the fifteen I wanted, I ended up with ten or eleven that I felt I could use." It is my guess that anyone who wanted to know Coach Raymond's opinion about his Olympic teams could get his opinion, without him ever being specific about where the problems were.

While he is unwilling to compare specific players he has coached over a 40+ year period, he was willing to tell me what made some of the players he saw over those years special. Carol Spanks, who was a consistent opponent over her entire best of the best career, earned this praise from Raymond, "The thing that people don't realize about Spanks was that she was capable of getting in position on opposing hitters and players and just making the play, whereas some others playing shortstop had to really work to get there. And Spanks had the mentality to get into position before the play happened. A lot of coaches and ball players never saw that. That was one of the things that made her so great: the ability to make the defensive play before it happened."

With respect to Joan Joyce, his most famous early athlete, he had this to say: "Joannie had a natural ability to do things and it showed itself. She was a championship bowler, champion basketball player, champion softball player. She made her mark in golf." Raymond referred to Joyce as "The Big Train" because like Baseball Hall of Famer Walter Johnson, Joyce wanted the ball, especially in big games.

Then there was Sue Enquist: "Susie Enquist could have been one of the all-timers as a player, but she opted for surfing. She stayed five years with me, then she decided she wanted to be a surfer. But in the five years that she was with us she proved to be one of the outstanding outfielders in the game. She really enjoyed surfing as opposed to softball but she had the ability and the knowledge and it proved itself when she became a coach."

Doing Good by Being Good

Since much of this section has been precisely identified by Dot Richardson's recollections of her coach earlier in the chapter, you might also be interested in how Ralph helped Dot regarding career choices. When speaking about Dot he said: "I remember the intensity she brought to the game." Raymond wanted her to succeed in athletics and to become a doctor.

Dot recalls, "I remember Coach Raymond telling me, 'Dot, be different. Go and do something else beyond softball. Don't let softball get in the way of your profession as a doctor.'"

Lisa Fernandez also made a huge impression on her coach: "The thing with Lisa was that she wasn't afraid to work at her game. She went from morning till night. It just wasn't one or two hours – she was constantly at it. I can remember seeing her going to the gym at 10pm to work out."

Ralph Raymond has had his share of attention and recognition over the years. When he speaks about priorities he is eloquent: "The two most important things that I stress to my teams – number one was team and number two was game. You have to put these before all the notoriety and accolades that will eventually come your way."

Raymond, who has had two quadruple bypass operations, and his wife, the former Mary Irene Morello (an R.N.) have been married 62 years and have seven children (four boys, three girls), 14 grandchildren and two great grandchildren.

One of his daughters, Kathy Ermilo (née Raymond) told the *Worcester Magazine* in 1993 that, "He brought us up like a ball team. A lot of discipline but a lot of love." So Raymond has had two families, his family at home and the kids who comprised his softball family through more than four decades. Ralph Raymond cares about both of his families and we are all better off for having his example of what can happen when respect and reverence for human accomplishment come together.

Dr. Dot Richardson listened to USA two-time Olympic Coach Ralph Raymond, who told her: "Don't let softball get in the way of your profession as a doctor." (Photo courtesy USA Softball)

Baseball Hall of Famer Ted Williams faced Joan Joyce, then 21 years-old, in an exhibition for the Jimmy Fund in 1961. (Photo courtesy of Joan Joyce).

Chapter 13

JOAN JOYCE
"THE ATHLETE'S ATHLETE"

Grace Under Pressure

In the preceding chapter, Ralph Raymond provided a brief sketch of his top pitcher, Joan Joyce, whom he called "the Big Train" after Baseball Hall of Famer Walter Johnson, whose career included over 4,000 strikeouts. Later we will expand on the many athletic gifts that were part of Joan Joyce's repertoire, but for now look at the photo to the left and you will see a remarkable picture of two athletes who have agreed to face each other in a hitting and pitching exhibition. Hitting comes before pitching here because the Boston Red Sox soon-to-be Hall of Famer, Ted Williams, had recently retired and had been called upon by the Waterbury police department to help raise money for "the Jimmy Fund," a cancer charity.

On Aug. 5, 2011, the 50th Anniversary of the hitting-pitching exhibition, Dave Scheiber went down to talk to Joan and others who were a part of the exhibition for a News and Opinion article on ESPNW.com*. To give a sense of Joan's reputation among those who knew her at the time, her catcher,

Copyright © ESPN.com. Reprinted with permission by ESPN

Career Highlights
(Pitcher, First Base, Coach)

•*1974, Led USA to ISF World Championship in
    Stratford, Conn. First time USA won the event*
•*Named an ASA All-American 18 consecutive years*
•*Compiled 67-10 pitching record in 18 ASA Nationals*
•*Member of 12 ASA National Championship teams*
•*Overall career of 753 wins and 42 losses*
•*Compiled 429-27 record with the Brakettes and 80-6
    with the Lionettes*
•*Struck out 5,677 batters in 3,397.1 innings with
    Brakettes and had a 0.21 ERA*
•*Won outright or shared MVP Award in ASA National
    Championship eight times*
•*1974 was first woman honored with a Gold Key from the*
•*Connecticut Sports Writers Alliance*
•*Has been inducted into nine Halls of Fame including
    ASA (1983), and ISF (1999)*
•*1994, Named Head Coach of Florida Atlantic University*
•*Has college coaching career record of 714-403
    (.643 winning %)*
•*Led Connecticut Falcons to four World Series titles in
    women's pro league*

*(See other source material for statistics in USA National
Volleyball, USA National Basketball and LPGA Golf)*

Micki Stratton's husband Johnny, told Dave the following: "Joan Joyce is the greatest player who ever played the game. She dominated the sport for 24 years…But she was tops at everything – volleyball, basketball, bowling, shooting pool, ping pong, cards – it didn't make a difference. She'd always beat you."

The upshot of this story is that Joan Joyce and Ted Williams got together one night in front of 17,000 fans in Waterbury, Connecticut with Joan clearly getting the best of it. By now you should be aware that this book is as much or more about how and why the best of the best went about doing whatever they accomplished than it is about the good fortune of a particular outcome. Go back to the picture. Is Ted Williams pleasantly looking at Joan Joyce, or showing any particular signs of friendliness? Williams was an ace fighter pilot during both WW II and the Korean War whose 20/10 eyesight (he could see at 20 feet away what an average person could see at 10) was behind his reputation as having the best eyes ever to play baseball. Does Joan see the possibility of going against one of the top 5 hitters who ever played Major League Baseball as a fate worse the death? How would you describe her demeanor? He is in his 40s when the picture was taken – she is 21. Let the games begin.

The next paragraphs are taken directly from Scheiber's story:

"So they called me and asked if I'd go with them, and I said yes," Joyce said. "They had me bring my uniform, glove and spikes, and Ted set up a time in the morning for me to pitch to a bunch of the counselors, and also him. At the time, I was having a little problem with my arm – we were getting close to going to the national tournament and it was a concern. I'd get this shooting pain."

But Joyce went with the group anyway, and she pitched, while trying to not overdo it because of her arm injury.

"Some of them hit the ball, some didn't – and then Ted came up, and he hit the ball, too," she said. "I don't know if I was just

being too careful or what. But afterward, we were walking up a hill to have lunch with him and discuss having him come to Waterbury. He's walking in front of me and halfway up there, he stops and turns around to me and goes, 'How'd you throw that curveball?'"

Joyce took the ball from her glove and demonstrated how she gripped and spun it.

"He looks at me and says, 'Girls shouldn't know that.' I looked at him and I said, 'This girl does know that.'"

Maybe Williams liked the way she had stood her ground. Minutes later over lunch, he agreed to take part in the fund-raiser, and to bat against Joyce as part of it.

Remember that this story dates from 1961 and William's comments about what women are supposed to know and do are not meant to be either insulting or congratulatory. They are a reaction to seeing for the first time something that he didn't know existed. Later shocks will follow. Let's get back to Dave Scheiber's narrative:

The August date was set, and Williams arrived for the big luncheon to kick off the festivities. Joyce's coach sat next to the star and made small talk. Among the things Williams told him was that he didn't like high, tight inside pitches.

"So my coach comes up to me and tells me this," Joyce says. "I looked at him and said 'Ted is just trying to set me up, because he knows you'll come back and tell me.' So I said, 'He's not gonna get a high, inside pitch. He's got the best eyes in baseball. If he's going to hit me he's going to have to hit my drop ball, which is down and away.'"

That night, a parade preceded the much-publicized exhibition. Dom DiMaggio, Joe's younger brother and a seven-time All-Star for the Red Sox, and a former American League pitcher named Spec Shea showed up to take part. Williams took Joyce aside and asked her to take it easy on DiMaggio, because he couldn't see out of his left eye.

"He said, 'Just warm up and let him hit, then you can throw hard to me,' so I accommodated him and Dom hit the ball pretty well," she said.

For those of you tracking our themes of Grace Under Pressure, Growing Smarter, and Doing Good by Being Good, a number of lessons stand out from these exchanges between Joyce and Williams.

First, whatever Williams expected when he went to help a charity out has been complicated by the appearance of a curve ball thrown by an unexpected source. From Joan's perspective, her assertive answer to his questions about her right to have such a pitch intrigued him sufficiently to set up the exhibition. During the exhibition, one of the most famous intimidating presences at home plate tried to get a game-playing competitive edge by asking not to be thrown into the briar patch of those terrible high and tight pitches close to his 20/10 vision.

It was Joan and not her coach who saw the gambit and took it as a ploy to give an edge to the man who referred to himself as the best hitter who ever lived. She set her strategy based on these two parts: One, Williams would get some high and tight rise balls, but they will be too far above the strike zone for him to want to swing; two, he would be getting a strict diet of low and away heat, dropping off the table for good measure. Considering that Joan is only 21, it is her remarkable "savvy" that has made this contest as much a chess match as it is a test of pure hitting and pitching skills.

There is something that should be said about Ted Williams: he had nothing to gain and potentially something to lose about getting into this exhibition. He might have said something like that his back was hurting, so they should take it a bit easy and they'd give the fans something to cheer about. Instead he asked the favor of treating Dom Dimaggio as a retired player helping a cause who deserved a respectful and caring at-bat. But when it came to the main event the 17,000 had come to the stadium to see, no quarter was expected or given.

Back to Dave Scheiber's story:

"I had him up there for 10-15 minutes, and he fouled off three pitches," she said. I gave him some rise balls, but they were out of the zone and I knew he wouldn't swing at those 'cause his eyes were so good. Then I went to my drop."

He swung – and missed – and missed repeatedly.

"You know, I had really mixed emotions about it, she said. " I thought 'Maybe I should have let him hit a couple – just for the show.' But I was too competitive. I've always said if my mother put a bat in her hands and came up to hit, I'd have to strike her out too."

The Joyce-Williams exhibitions received broad attention and she credits it more than any other string of championships for bringing her to the nation's attention. Somewhat later a mini-repeat was held with the same result. As the title of Scheiber's article, "The Best Williams Ever Faced," suggests, when asked later in life whom the best pitcher he ever faced was, Williams responded with no hesitation, "You won't believe it, but it was a girl."

When I first watched Joan Joyce play, my reaction was that this was a woman playing with younger girls. She seemed to be able to do anything she wanted on that field. When she wasn't throwing her unique slingshot delivery, she was playing a flawless first base or leading her National Championship team in batting. As a pitcher she wanted her team to know that whatever happened out there behind her, she would make it right. Nobody would score. Joan's on-the- mound saying was "Next Pitch" – nothing can be done about the one that got away. The pitch after this one is way too far in the future. I've got the ball and with full concentration on this pitch, that ought to be enough.

Growing Smarter

If you can put together a ton of talent that can be directed at a championship level to any game or sport you finds interesting, then the only missing parts are desire and work ethic. When those three elements come together in the same person, legendary achievements become the norm. Joan Joyce lived near the Brakettes, and her father was associated with fast pitch softball. At an early age the boys and their fathers in the Little League she wanted to play in decided that her gender made her unfit for Little League.

This is well before Title IX and consistent with a point of view about female athletics based on the idea that if we can't make it go away, then at least we can make sure that it is separate and given less attention. Joyce credits Williams with helping to change that notion, but more than ten years before their encounter she was trying to have fun without getting too many upset by her extra skill sets.

One of her solutions, familiar to many other athletes, was to become a practicing group of "one," shoveling basketball courts in the winter and amusing herself for hours at a time practicing and rehearsing what she would need to do later in games. Her home had a back garage wall on which she painted the strike zone rectangle. After her mother grew weary of hearing the ball thud against the wall, Joan moved her target to a more flexible and forgiving location and kept it up until she moved to something else.

The two most imposing players of their time, as described by fellow players, coaches, and fans, are Joan Joyce and Lisa Fernandez. Sharron Backus, who has known both very well, describes Joan as having a more placid shell, whereas Lisa intends to intimidate. Both, however, believed in their heart of hearts that they had beaten you before the game began because they had out-worked you, had out-prepared for the game you were about to enter, and they just wanted to win more than anybody. Lisa is 5'6" tall, has gym-generated muscularity with relatively small hands (look back at her opening Chapter 1 picture holding the ball) while Joan is 5'10," a lanky superstar who had the presence of mind to believe that she could stand up to Ted Williams and make him blink. If you called either a "gym rat" you would not likely get an argument. They love to be at a place where they can find something to compete in and figure out ways to improve.

In softball for the Brakettes Joan compiled a 429-27 record and was named All-American 18 consecutive years. She also earned the MVP Award at the Women's Major Fast Pitch National Championship eight times. In 3,397.1 innings, Joan fanned 5,677 batters and hurled 105 no-hitters and 33 perfect games. She yielded only 102 earned runs in 476 games for an ERA of 0.21.

She played in 942 games, and holds the distinctions of having earned the second most career hits (940), second most career runs (457), second most doubles (22), second most triples in a career (67), second most RBI (529), most shutouts in a season (38), most no-hitters in championship play (8), longest game (29 innings) and second in most no-hitters in a season (13). She led the Brakettes in hitting six times 1960, 1962, 1967-69, 1973 and had a career batting average of .327. Her highest batting average was .406 in 1973.

Joyce's athletic achievements extend beyond the world of softball. Her basketball achievements include being named WBA All-American four times and AAU All-American three times and having scored a record 67 points in one game in 1964. Joyce served as player-coach for the Connecticut Clippers, competed in four Nationals, and was named to the All-East Regional team. Joyce holds the record for the lowest number of putts in a single round of PGA and LPGA golf, where she played on tour from 1977 to 1995.

Doing Good by Being Good

Fifty years after her historic encounter with Ted Williams, Joan Joyce believes that she did a good turn for her sport and for women's issues in the fight for gender equality in athletics. However, not one to rest on her laurels, you can find Joan Joyce today at her position as softball and golf coach for Florida Atlantic University in Boca Raton, Florida. She accepted the position in 1994 and has compiled an impressive 714-403 record for her softball team. In the early part of 2011, she passed the 700 win total as the 2011 team finished with a 34-25 record. She has never had a losing season.

Despite losing in the Atlantic Sun conference final to Louisiana-Lafayette, 8-0, Joan said her team "was a lot of fun to coach this year. I had a team where there were no issues. They played hard and I am telling you it probably was one of my least talented teams."

Joan considers herself a fair coach. "I want them to have fun. When I have to be tough I'll be tough. It's a long season. The kids start in August, lifting and running and doing individual work. As soon as January rolls around, they come back for their second semester. They play from then until they are done with school. It's a long, long season. They have cut the season to 56 games, but if you go back three or four years [to when Joyce played ASA Women's Major Fast Pitch for the Brakettes and Lionettes] we were playing 65-70 games. That was our summer schedule."

Although the game has changed a lot during her 50+ years of being a major example of best of the best conduct on and off the field, if you ask Joan about fast pitch softball, the hitter in her immediately comes out. "I like it. What's there not to like about it? They moved the pitchers back so there is a lot of hitting. I think it's a good game." And when it's played or coached by one of the best who ever put on spikes or sneakers or whatever the contest called for, it has been something special.

Two ASA Hall of Famers, Joan Joyce (left) and E. Louise Albrecht. Joyce was inducted in 1983 and Albrecht two years later.

Sharron Backus not only was an outstanding college and pro coach but she earned ASA All-America honors six times during her outstanding career as a player. (Photo courtesy UCLA Sports Information)

Chapter 14

SHARRON BACKUS
"DYNASTY DESIGNER"

Growing Smarter

Sharron Backus belongs in this book twice, as do some of the other players of her era who first made a name for themselves as ASA standouts and later made a second career as Division I champion softball coaches. There is a bit of an arbitrary quality putting the early career under the heading of "Growing Smarter," because these are women who had a knack for growing as smart as they needed to be, first to become outstanding players and second to take their team through the college maze of obtaining (as dictated by Title IX legislation) the same support for the women's programs that the men's programs enjoyed. Sometimes the politics of getting administrators to do the right thing for the fledgling women's programs required more skill and tact than what was needed to play a good season and win a championship. But Sharron and the others who follow in this section were known for their ability to make others keep their word even when they didn't want to.

It is always more fun to begin where some representative of the sports society at large discovers that there is among them an eight-year-old girl with a golden arm. Here is Sharron's story: "One weekend, there were some kids where my grandmother

Career Highlights
(Shortstop and Coach)

- *Coached UCLA to national titles in 1982, 84, 85, 88, 89, 90, 92, 95*
- *Compiled record of 854-173-3 coaching Bruins from 1975-1996*
- *Led UCLA to an AIAW national title in 1978*
- *Inducted into ASA National Softball Hall of Fame (1985),*
- *Women's Sports Foundation Hall of Fame (1993), National Fast Pitch Coaches Hall of Fame (1991)*
- *Coached 29 All-Americans during her career including Dot Richardson, Debbie Doom, Sue Enquist and Lisa Fernandez*
- *Backus named six-time ASA All-American, playing from 1961-1975*
- *Played for Whittier Gold Sox, Orange Calif. Lionettes and Raybestos Brakettes*
- *Member of five ASA national championship teams with Raybestos Brakettes from 1969-1975 and one with the Gold Sox, 1961*
- *Compiled a .292 batting average (276 for 946) during her seven years with the Brakettes and appeared in 13 ASA National Championships overall*
- *1974, was a member of the gold medal-winning USA team represented by the Brakettes in the ISF World Championship. USA won this event for the first time.*
- *Member of the Connecticut Falcons, who won pro World Series four years in a row.*
- *Named WPF/WPSL Coach of the year in 1998 for Orlando Wahoos after winning first half and second half titles.*

lived, where there was also a big elementary school with a big wide-open field. We would meet there, pick teams, and play softball or football. My first softball coach, Ed Patrick, was driving by and he saw me throw a football. I was the quarterback. He said, 'Oh, my gosh.' He stopped, asked me over, and introduced himself to me. He wanted to know if I would be interested in playing softball. That was the beginning."

Backus played for the Anaheim Toppers and by age 15 had landed a spot on one of the top women's Major fast pitch teams, the Whittier Gold Sox of Whittier, California. The Gold Sox won the national title the first year Sharron played on the team, going 5-1 and knocking off the renowned Raybestos Brakettes. The Gold Sox defeated the Brakettes 2-1 in 19 innings to win the title. Joan Joyce pitched 18 and two thirds innings while Lou Albrecht was the winning pitcher. Joyce allowed only 5 hits – Backus and Coleen Riley had two hits each. Backus, at 15 years of age, batted fifth; right-fielder Riley batted lead-off.

Reflecting on that national championship, Backus said, "Joan Joyce was one of a kind. I saw Joan play and played against her. It was my first national championship. I didn't know anything – I was just a young rookie. These Brakettes, I didn't know who they were. We went up against the phenomenal Joyce. I didn't know Joan Joyce yet, but Joanie learned who we were. She kept throwing that rise ball and I would tomahawk it over my head and get a base hit or two."

Backus had the reputation for sure hands and a strong throwing arm playing either shortstop or third base. That year she earned second-team All-American honors. Sharron played for the Gold Sox for two more years before switching to the Orange, California Lionettes. For Backus it was "an evolution of friends and the people I played with. I enjoyed it. As long as it was enjoyable I stayed in the same place. It was hard when I left Whittier because I was young. Then I went to Orange, then the

Brakettes."

Going to the Lionettes enabled Sharron to play with top players Carol Spanks and Shirley Topley, both members of the ASA Hall of Fame. Backus starred for the Lionettes from 1964-1966 and earned first-team All-American honors twice. In her three years with the Lionettes she batted .285, .293, and .263. Leaving Whittier was particularly difficult: "It was a real hard time for [Whittier manager] Margo Davis because [Orange and Raybestos] were our arch enemies. But my connection was the attachment to the people. I couldn't take Margo and [assistant coach] Johnny Brooks with me. I enjoyed playing with Joan, Shirley, Carol and everyone involved."

Reflecting on Sharron's career with the Lionettes, Spanks said, "Sharron Backus was an excellent ball player. She was an outstanding shortstop, and in the few years she played with the Lionettes she did a fine job in left field, too. She wasn't one you could take a breath on when she came to bat, either…she could hit the long ball. She was a real mainstay on the Whittier team she played for. Her defensive skills really helped solidify that team."

Backus finished her ASA career playing seven years (1969-1976) with the Brakettes and posting a .292 batting average. She was a member of five national championship teams (1971-1975) and also played in the 1974 ISF World Championship in Stratford, Connecticut with the USA, represented by the Brakettes, capturing the gold medal – a first for the USA after having finished second twice before. She batted .296 in the ISF World championship and finished that year with a .318 batting average.

Grace Under Pressure

If you were going to design a lifetime of experiences that would prepare you for the rigors of starting a Division I athletic program from the ground up, you couldn't look to a better model than the ones that Sharron Backus had. From the age of 8, she was selected to be the athlete she already was. By 15, she was a major cog in a women's Major team that took on and beat the reigning best of the best, including its legendary pitcher, Joan Joyce. For the next ten or so years, she bounced around the best three teams that softball had to offer, making friends along the way and learning what each dominant player brought to the game. But mostly, she developed a sense of what it meant to be on different teams with the same exact goal – become national champions.

In 1969, Sharron Backus graduated from Cal State Fullerton, majoring in physical education and art design. She was teaching high school in 1975 when Judith Holland asked her to be the head softball coach for UCLA. Holland had seen Backus play and recalled that she was one of the best shortstops in the game. Backus was teaching physical education at a high school in Anaheim, California when she was hired by UCLA and continued to teach PE for a couple of years afterwards. At least one other pioneer coach, Carol Spanks at Cal Poly, did the same thing for the first few years until this new way of making a living took a hold and could support a full-time salary.

Backus taught her PE classes in the morning, then drove to UCLA to conduct practice and coach games in the afternoon. The job, according to Holland, paid around $1,500. Backus had coached at the high school level for seven years. According to Sharron, "It was a natural next step. I had coached every sport except softball in high school…track, field, swimming, basketball, and volleyball. I had played softball all those years competitively, so I knew the game. Basically, it was an easy transition to implement the skills involved with your personality and techniques.

"You have innate abilities within your personality, which are spawned as you grow from experience. I feel like I had the best experiences from the very beginning – the foundation established and built by Margo Davis, then I went to different teams: Bill Arlington and Frank Ciarelli with the Lionettes and then, of course, I went with Ralph Raymond."

For those of you aware of our three pillars, a discussion of what wisdom Backus took from each coach could also have been placed under the heading of "Doing Good by Being Good." From Margo Davis, Backus gained a sense of proper discipline and structure, perseverance, and repetition, repetition, repetition. On Frank Ciarelli, she says, "He built the confidence the Lionettes had. The players would suck up confidence like a sponge – you knew you were good because you played for the Lionettes. But with that came responsibility and professionalism. It didn't matter how old you were, you conducted yourself in a certain manner." From Ralph Raymond, Backus took toughness and endurance. Raymond taught his players to stay positive and respect the opponent, but remain consumed with their own execution and their own game – if you did that, "winning would take care of itself."

The most dominant player personality on UCLA's team in the beginning was Sue Enquist. Said Backus, "I took after Ralph's idea of quiet thunder. There needed to be a roar, a burn, and a fire within your belly. I felt like I had that as a player and I wanted to hang onto that as a coach. So I tried to have that kind of demeanor. Not intimate, but the kids respected the fact that they knew I had an explosion. They either had to execute or have the same intensity in their execution, if they didn't get it right. Sue wanted to win as strongly as I did, but it came out in a different way…She has that desire at a very, very high level, yet is very positive about it. I think we complemented each other."

In 1978 UCLA won its first national title, going 31 - 3. Enquist was the team's star player in center field and led the AIAW National Championship in batting. After Enquist graduated, Backus convinced her to remain at UCLA as an assistant coach. She was an assistant coach until Backus retired and was head coach until she herself retired in 2006.

Doing Good by Being Good

Sharron's situation is somewhat unique because she did not come from a sports family. "I was the only one that played ball in our family," said Backus, "except for my grandmother, who had been a ball player. My parents supported me and drove me to games until I got old enough to drive. My dad (Clarence, nicknamed Curly) played catch with me only once because I threw the ball so hard that it bruised his hand. He said, 'I can't do this anymore. You are going to have to find somebody else.'"

In her career at UCLA, Backus compiled a record of 847-167-3 and led the Bruins to nine national championships; compiling a record of 188-32 in post-season play. The Bruins reached the WCWS in 14 of 15 seasons and won eight NCAA crowns including three straight in 1988, 1989, and 1990. She coached five players who won the Honda Award – a total of eight times in twelve years – and one player, Lisa Fernandez, who won the Honda Broderick Cup as the outstanding college female athlete.

Backus has been inducted into the ASA Hall of Fame, the UCLA Athletic Hall of Fame, the Women's Sports Foundation Hall of Fame, the Fullerton College Hall of Fame and the NFCA Hall of Fame.

She has had a unique position in the history of women's softball because of her love of the people who have played it. Starting on the West Coast, gaining experience from the two top

West Coast rivals and shifting to the East Coast counterparts, she has been exposed to the best examples of softball excellence of mind, body, and spirit available to anyone.

Listening to her describe such things as the importance of balancing her discipline against the positive motivational orientation of her long-time coaching partner Sue Enquist suggests that she would even take the step of reducing her own authority if it meant giving her team a better chance to win. That means that she was able to go beyond seeing herself as the most important member of the team, as some coaches are inclined to do, and move to the higher position of finding the best ways to achieve consistent winning play over many years. For this she deserves the title of "Dynasty Designer" because it was done by plan, with the ability to benefit from requisite variety.

Sharron Backus coached UCLA to eight NCAA national titles from 1975-1996. She also led the Bruins to the AIAW national title in 1978. (Photo courtesy of UCLA Sports Information)

Sue Enquist was UCLA's first NCAA softball All-American, 1978, and was involved with 11 national championships as a coach and player at UCLA. (Photo courtesy UCLA Sports Information)

Chapter 15

SUE ENQUIST
"SOFTBALL'S TOP MOTIVATOR"

Grace Under Pressure

Ask Natasha Watley, the four-time All-American and two-time Olympian about her UCLA coach, Sue Enquist, and she will smile and tell you that if Sue told her she could walk on water she would be looking for a place to prove the coach right. It's all about mindset, you see, and Sue Enquist is credited by friends and foes alike with a powerfully effective mindset. Look across at her picture, whichever one we selected, and you will see a person having fun on the field, whether in a game or getting ready for one. Sharron Backus, her predecessor and later co-coach at UCLA, likened her to an inexhaustible source of energy – always on the go, positive, upbeat, enthusiastic, and focused. There are many driven competitors, but few can communicate a continuous sense of a positive, engaging will. Others can get dragged down by obstacles. One of the secrets (not so secret if you talk to her) of Sue Enquist's success on and off the field is that she loves the puzzles and predicaments that the game presents.

When Sue's new standout catcher, Stacey Nuveman, joined the team, there was a problem she and Enquist had to address. As detailed in her own chapter, Stacey is one of the most powerful

151

Career Highlights
(Center Field, Coach)

- *Involved with 11 national championships as coach and player at UCLA – 1,314 wins overall.*
- *Only person to win an NCAA Softball national championship as a head coach and a player.*
- *Ranked Number One; winning percentage and national championship titles-NCAA Division One*
- *2003 C. Vivian Stringer Coaching Award by the United States Sports Academy*
- *2000 UCLA Jersey #6 retired*
- *Top 100 20th Century Bruins-UCLA magazine (all sports male and female)*
- *Was UCLA's first All-American (1978), after being named All-Region in 1976, 77, and 78.*
- *Member of four ASA National Championship teams, 1976, 77, 78 and 1980 with the Raybestos Brakettes*
- *Served nine seasons as assistant under Sharron Backus*
- *Three-time Pac-10 Coach of the Year, 1995, 99 and 2006*
- *Compiled coaching record of 857-175-1 (.835 winning percentage)*
- *Member of the 1978 ISF World team and 1979 USA Pan Am team*
- *One of eight softball coaches chosen to work with the 1996 USA National Team*
- *2008 Women's International Sports Foundation Hall of Fame*
- *2006 National Fastpitch Coaches Association Hall of Fame*
- *2000 San Juan Unified School District Hall of Fame*
- *1993 UCLA Athletics Hall of Fame*
- *1980 San Clemente High School Hall of Fame*
- *Named three-time ASA All-American, 1976, 1978, and 1981*

and effective hitters to ever play women's fast pitch softball at all levels of top competition. She is about six feet tall, very solidly built, with a home run hitter's swing and mentality. There is no pitcher in the world who Stacey thinks she can't take deep, so that all will remember the swing, the solid connection and the tape measure used to determine just how far the ball finally landed as she rounds the bases.

There is a countermeasure other teams can use against this offensive weapon. It's called the pitch around. The pitcher makes believe that Stacey will have a chance to swing but throws wide of the plate or high or low of the strike zone. The informal rules of the game suggest that providing an intentional walk (which is the safest way to get the batter to first base) every time the batter steps to the plate lacks a certain sportsmanship. It's a bit crass and to be reserved for obvious moments when the game is on the line, not during the first inning before one of the teams has even come to bat. So the thing to do that meets protocol is to pitch around and make believe the pitcher was trying to be "too fine" with pitches around the strike zone. The temporary loss of control has caused the walk rather than declaring the superiority of the batter.

After Stacey began to generate the best offensive numbers ever to occur in collegiate softball (refer to page 44) she had a period where she was given nothing to hit. Again, the prevailing wisdom in bat and ball sports is that the best offensive tactic is to never swing at bad pitches. That will throw your eye off when a good one comes along. Sue, knowing full well that a good pitch to hit was the equivalent of "wildness in the strike zone," created a non-traditional, off-the-chart, requisite variety solution that enabled Stacey Nuveman to become the best power hitter in the history of the game. As far and Sue and Stacey were concerned, a good pitch to hit was any pitch that Stacey could reach. Therefore, a 17-inch wide strike zone for the average player could be expanded 4 inches on either side to become a 25 inch strike zone and the normal armpits-to-knees height of the zone could be adjusted to whatever pitch Stacey felt she could put good contact on.

In the last chapter, Sharron Backus described the "tomahawk" swing to get two hits in the same championship day against Joan Joyce. There is a recent story about Derek Jeter and Yogi Berra that addresses when to go out of the strike zone and when not to. When Derek was approaching three thousand hits he started to swing at pitches over his head that he would have left alone if he had been less anxious. Yogi is reported to have come into the clubhouse after a game and mentioned that he saw Derek swing at and miss these high pitches. Jeter answered, "You swung at a lot of high pitches out of the strike zone."

"Yeah," said Yogi, "But I hit them."

Perhaps it was the fact that Sue Enquist was the first baseball player at her high school that encouraged her to try roads less traveled, but she was recognized by her peers as the coach whose quick mind saw everything. In fact, early in her career and as a member of the UCLA coaching staff, Enquist showed how valuable she was in helping to recruit Debbie Doom to UCLA. Said Enquist,"When I played I took pride in not striking out much. I faced her (Doom) three times (in the national tourney) that night and struck out all three times. I called Sharron (Backus) from the ball park on a pay phone. I think I still had my spikes on." Enquist was playing for the Raybestos Brakettes. Many people might have noticed, but how many would have had the confidence to call her former coach and tell her how she thought the school should spend a scholarship?

Growing Smarter

Sue Enquist has been the first high school baseball player in the state of California, a member of UCLA's first national championship team (1978 AIAW) where she led the AIAW World Series in batting with a .421 average. She twice led her team in batting and triples and three times in doubles. She was UCLA's first All-American, 1978, and its first scholarship softball player. She is the center fielder in this all-star group, and considering the way she could run, that might have been enough to carry most of the ground while players from other positions filled in, in left and right.

The baseball story was unusual. "I got into baseball because of my brother," said Enquist. "The greatest influence at that point was my brother's baseball coach, John Springman. And my brother literally taught me how to compete. I fell in love with the game, grew up playing it in the street. At the time we didn't have softball in San Clemente. So my introduction to softball was at Mission Viejo. I fell in love with the game and when I went to high school, I played both baseball and softball.

"I really enjoyed the difficulty of it, the challenge of it, the constant change from the individual competing against a pitcher to a teammate supporting other teammates and the team concept. It was because of the baseball opportunity that the door opened for UCLA. That's where I met my next greatest influence, Sharron Backus, who built the framework for UCLA. She literally approached the game with such humility and respect that I just copied everything she told us to do and in a three-year period, we built a 'bad news bears' team that had no uniforms into a national champion in 1978 in Omaha, Nebraska."

Reflecting on her early years at UCLA, Enquist said, "We would get to the field a couple of hours early, we would drag the field, water it and line it. We had no fence, no dugout, just a bunch of athletes. Next to our dugout, a single bench and your school buddies would be literally over your shoulder. It was quite interactive."

Before becoming the first UCLA player to be awarded a softball scholarship (1975-78), Enquist learned a valuable lesson about herself from Springman when she was playing baseball. "John Springman was the first coach who taught me that I was good at something. I will never forget that. We were having batting practice at San Clemente High School. We used to shag fly balls for about an hour and a half. One day he pulled me over and said, 'You're special and don't you let anyone tell you that you can't do this.' I just hung on to his words." On the high school JV, Enquist played outfield and shortstop. "My first year of UCLA softball was the second semester in high school of my senior year. I just graduated early. I went to high school for 3 ½ years."

While Sharron Backus was turning UCLA's program around, Sue Enquist had a front row seat. She was acutely aware of what both Coach Backus and UCLA Athletic Director Judith Holland brought to the program. In her words: "When Judith Holland came in during my sophomore year, our world was turned upside down in a positive way. We got meal money, we got cars to travel in, we got uniforms and we never looked back. And if you are talking about the history of college softball, you have to mention Judi Holland. Judi created the infrastructure to transfer AIAW over to the NCAA. She was a leader in that movement when Title IX created the law that was now going to be enforced at the collegiate level."

Again according to Enquist, "While playing college ball I also played summer ball for the Brakettes. Ralph Raymond was the individual who single-handedly taught me how to compete under pressure. I loved being on top, being in front. There was no pressure, it was a privilege. Ralph and John taught us that it's our game. The opponent, though we respect them, they are a mere formality to start OUR game, Raybestos Brakettes Softball."

So here we have two nearly simultaneous overlapping influences in the spring and summer, Backus and Raymond. Enquist noted, "It's important that Sharron Backus, through her demeanor, was able to make us feel so special. It didn't matter if we had support or uniforms. It was about your personal excellence and representing the institution. Although there was ample opportunity to whine and complain, we were led by someone who would have no part of that. And that was Sharron Backus."

Regarding the coaching transition between Backus and Enquist, here is how Sue Enquist saw their relationship: "Sharron created the backbone, the blueprint of the UCLA tradition. When I took over, I kept the same infrastructure and put my own fingerprint on it. Sharron taught me that it was never about the coach. That's a huge lesson in serving the game. We are most proud that we have more Bruin offspring coaching than any institution in the country.

"Backus was a person of few words but had high expectations. You are going to be successful with your inner confidence. External motivation is not predictable. You don't rely on other people to motivate you. Rely on yourself, your own commitment, because that is something you can rely on every day.

"Literally, player by player we just got better. She recruited the talent and brought up the team attitude. She made the game very simple for us. Ralph Raymond made the game simple. But like [her friend] John Wooden said, 'Mastery of the each of the fundamentals are the most important and demanding things an athlete can do – not just execution, but mastery of them.'"

Again, about her relationship with Wooden: "My career as a head coach at UCLA was hugely influenced by coach John Wooden. I had known him my whole career. He was instrumental in making sure that I kept balance and kept loving the game."

"My family upbringing taught me to stay positive. I got that from my mother as well as my enthusiasm for the game. My work ethic, my discipline, my drive, and my determination I got from my father and my brother. My faith that everything is going to be okay, I got from my sister. So I am the culmination of my family. But when I started to apply my personal principles, it was helpful to have Coach Wooden there to be my North Star."

"Perennial champions have a language within their head – they know how to manage the inside voice that they carry in a way that inspires people and a behavior that always denotes respect. They know how to hang on to assets to keep the balance, whether it's faith in God or whether it's faith in principles and ethics."

Doing Good by Being Good

In the 40 years or so that Sue Enquist has been a force in women's athletics, she has seen a number of good things as well as some about which she has concerns: "There are so many more opportunities for athletic women. The athlete today is well rounded, has a lot of different interests. I think that's important to articulate. Because of the advent of the scholarship at a very young age, everyone's motivation is about the scholarship. And when you change the focus from loving the game, participating in the game, and reaping the life lessons from the game, you switch the focus to being all about the scholarship."

"That brings out negative behavior in coaches, players, and parents. So now the parents have the pressure to move kids around teams and to coddle their children and do everything to make them happy. It's important as a parent to let your kids fail on the field. Failure is an important element in later success. You've got to have failure to re-calibrate yourself on how you need to go to the next level. So parents need to step up and be parents, in terms of having family principles and having performance boundaries. Kids need to step up. If your parents tell you something to do, go out there and try it as long as you are not being emotionally or physically abused. Let's find ways to serve the game so that kids can go out there and have fun and learn to better ball players."

One way that Sue Enquist has put her ideas into action is by launching a program called the Champion's Festival at the 2011 Women's College World Series. The Champions' Festival made its debut this year in conjunction with the Champion Series and is partially sponsored by the NCAA. The festival brought together former champion players and coaches to share their thoughts and experiences with players and fans of the sport of softball.

The initial turnout was positive and enthusiastic. "I think this is so exciting," said Leah O'Brien-Amico, a three time Olympic gold medalist and three time NCAA champion at Arizona. "For a long time, a lot of players have gone off individually or in small groups to share experiences and do talks and clinics. The Festival allows us to bring together so many of us who have been such a big part of our sport to give back to the game."

Judi Garman, head coach at Cal State Fullerton from 1980-1999 before going on to coach the Italian National Team, said, "Having this Festival at the College World Series shows how softball is so much more than just a game. Softball has so much rich history in Oklahoma City, with much more history yet to be made. The Champions' Festival can make history of its own right along with it."

It is not surprising that one of softball's supreme motivators has decided to help her sport once again reach the top of its capacity. With such a noble cause and a list of champions to draw from, you have to salute Sue Enquist, whose reverence for the game matches her extraordinary career. And keep your eye out for new developments regarding this important group effort because for Sue, team is the only way to think about softball.

Carol Spanks earned ASA All-America honors 13 times during her career before coaching at the University level for 20 years at Cal Poly Pomona and UNLV. (Photo courtesy of Stormy Irwin)

Chapter 16

CAROL SPANKS
"GRACE AND STYLE"

Growing Smarter

As you can tell by looking at Carol Spanks' playing picture, we have gone back to the era of Joan Joyce and the satin shorts uniforms. When Carol began playing in 1951 and in the latter half of the 1950's, when she reached the Major-level Orange County Lionettes, that is the way that women who wished to play were expected to outfit themselves. But this is about 25 years before Women's NCAA softball and at least 15 before Title IX legislation. Women who wanted to play ball found other women who wanted to play ball and had a great time for the love of the sport.

What makes Carol Spanks so special is that she doesn't consider herself special. However, here is what Sharron Backus, a younger teammate and opponent of hers, had to say: "She was such a classy player, so good and talented physically. She was a classy teacher of the game. I respected her so much on the field, the way she carried herself and played. I wanted to be just like her. There are few of those types in the game – not only the physical, but the emotional and professional type that Carol displayed. She was one of a kind."

Career Highlights

(Shortstop, Pitcher and Coach)

- Played in 19 National Championships; named ASA All-American 13 times
- Member of four ASA National Championships, 1962, 65, 69, and 1970
- Erv Lind Award Winner 3 times (1968-70) as Outstanding Defensive Player in the ASA National championship
- In 686 games with the Lionettes batted .322
- 16 times named to the Pacific Coast Women's League all-star team
- 5 time Pacific Coast Women's League batting champion
- Pitching record for Lionettes 122-28
- 15 seasons as Head Coach at Cal Poly Pomona, 577-310 and 5 ties record
- Led Cal Poly Pomona to 11 post season appearances (3 AIAW – 8 NCAA)
- 5 Cal Poly Pomona teams advanced to NCAA WCWS
- In 1979 and 1988, finished 3rd in NCAA WCWS
- In 1985 and 1990 named Big West Conference Coach of the Year
- 1987, Head Coach of gold medal Pan American Games team
- 1985, ASA All-Star team gold medal coach in the South Pacific Classic
- 1995-2000 Associate Head Coach, UNLV

Joan Joyce considered Carol Spanks one of the best hitters of her era, not just because she was able to hit Joan with some regularity, but because Joan, through all the times they faced one another, could not find a weakness in Carol's plate coverage. And remember, Joan Joyce is the pitcher who figured out at age 21 the most effective way to pitch to the rest of women's softball and Ted Williams.

Ralph Raymond, however, spoke of an even higher level of softball savvy, one of his winning principles, when he described Carol's ability to anticipate plays before they occurred on the field and be moving in the direction of the ball before it struck the bat. You might have heard the phrase "off with the crack of the bat" – according to Ralph, Carol was able to detect something in the pitcher's pitch characteristics and the batter's preparation which combined to put Carol in position to have an easy play, time after time. What was so interesting to Coach Raymond was how others failed to detect what she was able to do. They gave her credit for being fast, which she was. He gave her credit for what Dr. Dot Richardson, the next generation's "Best of the Best" shortstop, refers to as "being one with the ball."

Look over Carol's ASA Hall of Fame career and you will notice, almost as an afterthought, that she compiled a 122-28 record as a pitcher. She will admit to throwing a hard down ball but gives all credit for her pitching achievements to her ASA Hall of Fame catcher, Nancy Ito. According to Spanks, she just threw whatever Nancy Ito told her to; there was never a reason to have to think on her own.

Spanks graduated from Pasadena City College (1954-56) where she starred in four sports before completing her final two years at UCLA (1958). Reflecting on her career, Carol said, "As a player of ASA ball, at that time there was no collegiate softball competition for those of us ball players. We had no scholarships and there was no pro ball. So we all played for the love of it and it seemed that many players on the major teams stuck with their teams for many years. We had players on the teams who were teenagers and those who were nearing 40. The blend was wonderful…rookies learned from the veterans and the veterans were dealing with the issues of younger players.

"The quality of teams was at the highest. The ultimate goal of our sport was winning a very tough regional to qualify for a national championship. If you were fortunate enough to be on a team that did go to the nationals and your team did well enough in that tournament, players on the team who did well could make the All-Star team. It was a big deal to go the following year to the home of the defending champion and compete against them in a four game series. Those All-Stars who were on the championship team played with their own team and spots were filled by the second team All-Americans.

"When college ball became a part of athletic programs and I got into coaching, it was like a dream come true. I had gone into physical education because of my love of sports and now there was a venue for continuing my career specializing in the sport of my choice…softball. What could be better?

"As the sport advanced and grew, eventually the Major program suffered somewhat. Classifications now existed at the ASA level so it was no longer AAA, AA, and A levels, but rather by age. Kids began playing with the idea of getting a scholarship to a university and the changes were good in some ways, but the ways of the game I knew dwindled and now are almost defunct."

Grace Under Pressure

Before we go to a few memories that stand out today from her playing days, let's look at a brief synopsis of her marvelous career: In 19 ASA competitions, she was named an All-American 13 times. She was a member of four national championship teams, 1962, 1965, 1969, and 1970 playing for the Orange, California Lionettes. During the period1966-1975 Spanks led the Lionettes in batting six times and was runner-up twice, compiling a .322 batting average in 686 games. She received the Erv Lind Award as the outstanding defensive player in the ASA Women's Major Fast Pitch National Championship three times (1968-1970). In 1970, the Lionettes represented the USA in the second Women's Fast Pitch Championship in Osaka, Japan. The Lionettes lost to Japan in the championship game. Carol batted .303 in the championship.

"As I reflect back on my playing days there are a few instances which immediately stand out and give me cause for a smile or a head shake," said Carol. "The first to come to mind was back in 1962. As was typical then, the Orange Lionettes once again qualified for the national tournament which was to be held that year in Stratford, Connecticut. We had a good team, not one loaded with a lot of individual talent, but we were coming off a good season of play. The nationals were a tough tournament to qualify for…especially coming out of the Southern California area where there were about four very competitive teams vying for one spot. Fortunately Whittier had qualified automatically as defending champions which left a little less to contend with at the regionals.

"Per usual, the 18 or 19 teams were the best from all around the country playing in a double elimination tournament which would take place over nine days. We started the tournament with a win in our white uniforms. We had two sets: one basically orange and the other white. We came out the next day in our orange uniforms and lost. Thus began a string of superstitions amongst the team members which was not broken for the remainder of the tournament."

"We never wore our orange uniforms again nor did we wash them. Being made from heavy satin material, after a few days they stood on the floor of the rooms like little soldiers. We did, however, make sure they were ironed and neat."

"Long story short, we won the next seven games to be only the second team ever to win a championship coming out of the loser's bracket. But that's not the whole story. All the teams were competitive along the way but when we got down to the day before the finals, we had to meet and beat two of the toughest teams in the tournament led by two of the best pitchers in the game. [ASA Hall of Famer] Louise Mazzuca pitched for the Portland Florists and was a force to be reckoned with. She would definitely be considered one of the best ever to play the game. We won. Then came the Raybestos team led by the young phenom Joan Joyce, who many claim to be the best ever to pitch a ball, and if my recollection is correct, at that time from 38-feet. Not much time to pick up on a pitch from either Mazzuca or Joyce, with the speed they threw the ball. We won! I do believe we amazed ourselves – however, we weren't done yet. Final night rolled around and we had to beat the Whittier Gold Sox twice to capture the title. They were led by the tournament's MVP, Lou Albrecht, who pitched both games for the white ones...The Lionettes prevailed and for most of us it was our first national championship."

"You wouldn't find a person on that team who didn't believe that the dirty uniforms and the many other rituals we followed daily didn't play a major role in our success. What it did, in my opinion, was help us build confidence between each team member that made us actually believe we were going to win the entire thing. And when a team has that belief, it's difficult to have a different result regardless of the overall ability of the teams involved."

Typical of Carol Spanks, she described in a funny way how mindset and team unity can contribute to winning a string of games, all from the depths of the losers' bracket. What she forgot to mention was that it didn't hurt having the perennial All-Star shortstop and one of the best hitters of that or any other era on your side.

Doing Good by Being Good

Carol Spanks received a bachelor's degree in physical education from UCLA, with a Special Secondary Teaching Credential. She also received a General Secondary Teaching Credential and Secondary Administrative Credential while doing graduate work at Whittier College. Between 1958 and 1978 Carol was a physical education teacher and coach in the Norwalk-LaMirada Unified School District.

Again in Carol's words: "In 1979 I had just quit my 20-year teaching career to do something else. I was working for a printing company in California when I got a call from some of the players on the Cal Poly Pomona softball team. I knew several of them, as they played for the Lionettes…most familiar to all would be Cindy Bristow and the eventual Stratford standout, Barbara Reinalda. They were desperate because their former coach, who also coached basketball at the university, was finding the two-sport assignment too much to deal with."

"My boss at the time said I could take the afternoons off to coach this team as long as I got my work done – which I did. I accepted a full time position after the initial year which was the beginning of my 15 year collegiate coaching experience at that university."

"The team agreed to have everything set up for practice when I got there and put away afterwards. And they did, all season long – I was very naïve and thought this would happen year in and year out; after the first year it never happened again. Anyway, what made this a highlight is that the team proceeded to win some 33 games without a loss, including a couple of ties. We went through the regionals successfully and advanced to the AIAW national championship in Omaha, Nebraska, where we finished 3rd."

"Cal Poly went to post-season play 11 straight years, tying the record with Fresno for consecutive appearances. The program eventually participated at the Division I level despite the remainder of Pomona's athletics being Division II. We had a total of five scholarships available, compared to ten and eventually eleven available to most Division I programs we competed against. I will always be grateful to this group of women for their efforts and success that first season. It sure made things a lot easier for me as coach in the ensuing years. The softball program was dropped in 1993 due to budgetary problems."

Carol finished her coaching career at UNLV where, for five years, she was the associate head coach. She retired in 2000 after 20 years at the university level. Carol went on to participate in a number of international Events. Her first head coaching job was in 1985 where she led the team to the gold medal at the South Pacific Classic. Then in 1987, she was head softball coach for the USA in the Pan Am Games in Indianapolis, bringing home the gold and going through the event undefeated.

"From my first organized playing experience in the mid 1950's until my retirement from the game as coach in 2000, I have had numerous wonderful experiences. The competition was terrific during my playing days and I loved every minute of being on the field. There were trying times along the way, to be sure, but as time goes by, one tends to recall the better moments."

What a graceful and gracious athlete and human being.

The 1969 season was one to remember for ASA Hall of Famers Shirley Topley (left) and Carol Spanks, both members of the Orange Lionettes. Topley coached the Lionettes (5-0) to their eighth ASA National title by beating the Raybestos Brakettes twice, 1-0 (14 innings) and 4-1 behind the fabulous pitching of ASA Hall of Famer Nancy Welborn. Topley, Spanks and Welborn all earned ASA All-America laurels. (Photo courtesy Stormy Irwin)

Besides playing amateur softball, Margie Wright played three years of professional softball (1977-79)

Chapter 17

MARGIE WRIGHT
"SENIOR STATESWOMAN"

Growing Smarter

If you are reading this book from front to back, it might be good to pause before you begin the story of Margie Wright, winningest fast pitch softball coach in Division I history. Her story is fairly common for young women who found that softball was the sport they enjoyed at a deep, fundamental level. What she uniquely did with it puts her in this book on a couple of lists: as player, coach, and activist who made a significant difference for generations of women who have benefited from her example.

We begin with a situation described earlier for other standout athletes: the girl finds that there is no such thing as organized girl's softball, signs up for Little League Baseball, and soon finds out that girls have been excluded from baseball for fear of injury. Look over at the picture of Margie pitching fastpitch for the St. Louis Hummers and you begin to wonder just who the local officials were afraid of getting injured. Margie clearly would have held her own. Because of the exclusion, Margie's mother and father "decided to have my dad start a city 'park' or 'rec' team with

Career Highlights
(Pitcher, Coach)

- *Winningest coach in Division I Softball with 1,421-519-3 record*
- *Second all-time winningest coach (by victories) in all of NCAA sports*
- *In 26 years at Fresno State has compiled 1,258-427-1 record (.747)*
- *Coached Fresno State to 1998 NCAA WCWS title, has finished runner up three times (1988, 1989, 1990), third place three times, fifth place three times*
- *Named USOC National Coach of the Year in Softball (1998)*
- *Coached Fresno State to 10 regional crowns and 26 consecutive NCAA postseason appearances*
- *In six years at Illinois State posted a 163-92-2 (.638) record while winning three state titles, two Gateway Conference regular season crown and one Gateway Conference title*
- *Member of 12 Halls of Fame*
- *Assistant coach for first USA Olympic Team in 1996*
- *Head Coach of the 1998 USA National team that won the ISF World Championship*
- *Head Coach of the 1995 USA Junior World Championship gold medal team*
- *USA National gold medal team assistant coach at 1995 Superball Classic*
- *Assistant coach of 1994 USA National team, which won the ISF World Championship with 10-0 record*
- *Assistant coach for gold medal 1991 USA Pan American Team*
- *Played women's Major fast pitch 31 years, Women's Professional Fastpitch 3 years*
- *Named ASA All-American four times*
- *Three-time U.S. Olympic Festival Head Coach*

two of my sisters and me, at age 10."

This led to ASA Class B and A teams and then on to Major Women's games against much older players. "Getting to face pitchers like Lorene Ramsey, Joan Joyce, and others was humiliating when I was barely big enough to swing a bat, but the failures and experience I obtained in those early years led me to a path of competing at the Major Women's and Professional levels for 34 years. I loved it and still do."

Here is how Margie Wright describes the early years: "There were no opportunities to play in elementary, junior high, or high school in organized sports, so I picked the only sport that was organized at that time: softball. There were no such things as pitching coaches like today so I spent hours practicing pitching against the back of the garage to the four targets my dad drew, and also throwing balls against the well platform in our side yard. My mom used to spend hours in the evenings hitting flies and grounders (about 500 a night) to my sisters, me, and all the neighborhood kids. Once my dad started our team, we all traveled in our family station wagon all over Illinois and Indiana. I know my family and others did without things sometimes so we could afford gas and had money for entry fees and food."

"After I moved up and my dad didn't have our team anymore, I had to cut corn and beans in the fields all week in order to have money to go play on another team two and a half hours away. Otherwise there was no money to eat on or for gas. Our sponsor was a car dealer and I was given an old car to drive back and forth to games, but I had to pay for the gas and oil in it. My family always came to watch but they couldn't leave as early as I had to because of work."

Let's follow Margie to college at Illinois State. "I had to take out a bank loan in order to go to college. I was the first in my family to go to college and my primary reason for going was I found out they played organized sports for women. I started college in the fall of 1970 and graduated in four years playing three sports year-round: field hockey, basketball and softball. Unfortunately, Title IX and the opportunity to receive an athletic scholarship did not come until I graduated. It took me twenty years to pay my loan back but it was well worth it. I got to fly on a plane for the first time in my life to play in the AIAW National basketball championships and crammed into a State station wagon to go to the College World Series three straight years, finishing 2nd in 1973."

"I didn't get to meet scholarship athletes because there were none. I got, however, to play against some of the best and the competition was pure and intense. I loved it. Every game was a challenge. I don't remember really feeling pressure because I was just willing to do whatever I could to win. Back then, we never thought about failure, we just wanted to beat whoever was on the other side of the field or court... I was a 'gym rat', the player who hung out in the gym or on the field every free minute I had. It was an experience of a lifetime."

Margie Wright described a bit more about lessons learned in this way: "There were so many lessons I learned from softball, like how to be a part of a team and how to fulfill my role – whatever it might be. I learned how to compete and conquer any obstacle that may get in my way. I have learned how to teach others about the values of life through a sport."

She also mentioned particular events that stood out during her playing days. "In the 1973 College World Series, my coach took me aside before playing the championship game against Arizona State University and asked if I could throw 4 or 5 different speeds to keep them off balance. Well, since they had knocked me out the day before, I said 'yes' and proceeded to practice throwing pitches I had never thrown in my life. We had to beat them twice in order to be the AIAW National Champion and we made a great run for it. We won the first game 4-0 (coach's strategy worked) and lost the championship game 4-3 in 16 innings. Being second was difficult to handle when we were so close, but the fight and strategy that we went into those games with was second to none."

Margie also goes on to rate winning the 1998 NCAA WCWS as her greatest college victory ever, and being one of the coaches for the gold medal winning Olympic team in 1996 with five of her collegiate players on that team as a thrill of a lifetime. Coach Wright also recalls what it felt like in 1996 to be hosting UCLA in Fresno State's new $5 million stadium with a standing-room-only crowd of 5,427. Four years later the attendance record was broken when they hosted Arizona with 5,724 in the stadium.

"These games were what women's softball should be about; great competition, great fans, and a great game venue to play it in. Those days rewarded years and years of fighting for Title IX and equality, as well as many days of marketing our program to our fans. What a reward!"

Grace Under Pressure

When asked about the most important influences on her career, Margie immediately pointed to her parents. "My parents had the biggest influence on me because they created the opportunity to play. They held me accountable for my desire to be the best I could be by helping me practice and work harder than anyone else. They convinced me that if I did, I could accomplish anything. They taught me to respect my coaches and teachers and do my best for them at all times. They taught me that sacrifice equals success and they taught me to win by being ethical and fair. I am forever grateful for their support.

"My college coaches really helped me, as well as my ASA coach in Moline, Illinois. They continued to teach me the message of my parents but their expectations of me became higher as they taught me the tools to achieve the higher goals." When asked about her opportunities in softball, Margie answered, "I've had the best opportunities a person could ever have in softball. My team and I had a no-hitter in the ASA National Championship when I was 36. Five years later my team and I finished fourth in the nation in 1993 at the ASA National Championship at the age of 41. My team and I, as a coach, have gold medals in the Pan Am Games, Junior World Championship, World Championship, and Olympic Games. As a coach, my team won the 1998 NCAA National Championship and I am currently the winningest coach in the NCAA. Thank you, softball, for allowing me to have players and teammates to help all of those accomplishments become realities."

Doing Good by Being Good

The Fresno State Bulldogs have an official athletic site that profiles Coach Margie Wright in her 27th season as head coach of the Fresno State softball program. The Wright profile extends for nine tightly jam-packed pages which takes up more space that any two of our profiles covers here – you can simply search for Coach Margie Wright's name on any search engine and it will lead you there. She has made an enormous contribution to the game thus far, with no signs of slowing down. But since the Bulldogs' website contains so many personal contributions and awards, it might be useful to take some headlines from that source.

First, Margie Wright is in 12 different Halls of Fame. In the fall of 2008, Wright and her 1998 NCAA National Championship team were inducted into the Fresno Athletic Hall of Fame. In the fall of 2006, Wright was inducted into the Fresno County Women Lawyers' Hall of Fame. She was also recognized by the National Women's Political Caucus of Fresno County with the "Promises to Keep Award." She was inducted into Illinois State University's Athletic Hall of Fame. The list goes on.

Sometimes doing good by being good is about positive events that generally help the sport and specifically help individuals. Coach Wright has been in the forefront of making sure that her student-athletes take advantage of the opportunities to develop their mental tools along with their physical on-the-field-tools. She has coached 53 All-Americans, 16 Academic All-Americans, four NCAA Postgraduate Scholarship award winners, four Honda Awards program softball finalists, eight professionals, 15 Olympians, two NCAA Top VIII award winners and two No. 1 professional draft picks.

However, there are times when it is also important to stand up and be counted in the presence of perceived inequalities. In this regard, Coach Wright has been the topic of news articles regarding her testifying in support of another faculty member and later settling her own suit against Fresno State out of court. Here is what was said in the news release dated July 11, 2008: "Fresno State and Head Softball Coach Margie Wright have reached an amicable resolution in their dispute over [employment issues]. 'I am pleased to have put these issues behind me,' said Coach Wright, 'I trust the administration's assurances of support including facilities improvements for the softball program. I look forward to continued success with the Fresno State softball program in the coming years.'"

For the pioneers in the college game, nothing was easy and nobody laid out a red carpet, but athlete-coaches like Margie Wright, Carol Spanks, Judi Garman and Sharron Backus, mostly fighting individual skirmishes in specific institutions, had the will and the commitment to make things better for the generations of women who deserved to be considered for college scholarships, decent playing conditions, and a fan-friendly venue. Put that together with magnificent athletes taught by dedicated teachers and the game's foundation was firmly established. Add some additional fan base through the possibilities inherent in televised events and if one is not too careful, it might be possible to forget just how this all happened.

"Senior Stateswoman" Margie Wright coached Fresno State to the NCAA national title in 1998 and was an assistant coach on the 1996 USA Olympic team. (Photo courtesy Fresno State)

Speaking to members of the Golden West JC softball team, Judi Garman compiled a record of 211-40 at the junior college including winning four JC national titles. (Photo courtesy Judi Garman)

Chapter 18

JUDI GARMAN

"FIRST FULL-TIME COLLEGE COACH"

Grace Under Pressure

Judi Garman played Major ball in the same era as Joan Joyce, Carol Spanks, and Sharron Backus, however, early on, she knew that she wanted to be a coach. According to Garman: "I chose to play on an outside basketball team with a famous coach so I could learn coaching techniques. I was a bench sitter in basketball so I wanted to observe the best coach available – took notes on every drill and how he handled things. I thought I would be a basketball coach, since there was no softball in college at the time (1962-1966) and I wanted to be well prepared."

After graduating from the University of Saskatchewan in 1966, Garman attended the University of Santa Barbara, California, graduating with a Master's degree in Kinesiology. While attending UC-Santa Barbara, Garman discovered negative attitudes toward women's athletics, well before the passage of Title IX in 1972. "I was shocked by the negativity toward women athletes. When I got the job at Golden West, I coached two teams, basketball and softball, and taught ten classes. The junior col-

Career Highlights
(Outfield, Coach)

- *At Cal State Fullerton compiled 913-376 (.708) coaching record from 1980-1999*
- *Coached Cal State Fullerton to 1986 NCAA WCWS*
- *Coached Fullerton to three NCAA WCWS runners up 1981, 83, 85*
- *Compiled overall coaching record of 1124-416 (.719)*
- *Won four National Junior College softball titles at Golden West*
- *Member of Canadian National Championship team 1969-70*
- *Member of Canada National Team, 1970*
- *Played in ISF World Championship in Osaka, Japan, 1970*
- *President of National Softball Coaches Association, 1990-91*
- *Member of Pan American Team coaching staff, 1979*
- *Coached three Honda Award winners*
- *Raised over $1,000,000 for college funding efforts*
- *Won two PCAA Conference championships 1986-87*
- *Won seven WCAA Conference Championships*
- *Won seven NCAA Regional championships*
- *Won Big West Conference title in 1993*
- *Inducted into Community College Hall of Fame, 1992*
- *Inducted into National Softball Coaches Hall of Fame, 1993*
- *Inducted into Cal State Fullerton Titan Hall of Fame, 2007*
- *President, National Softball Coaches Association*
- *Garman's sister, Lorraine, is a member of the LPGA Hall of Fame, being inducted in 2009. She was the first women teaching professional to have her own teaching center and is recognized as an expert in club fitting. She is recognized as an LPGA Master Golf Professional and is one of Golf Digest's top 20 women teachers.*

leges were well organized in the late '60s and early '70s. The university softball scene was mostly club teams."

"When Billy Moore was hired as the first full-time college basketball coach we hoped we would live long enough to see the same opportunity in softball. When Leanne Grotke decided to add softball (1979) at Cal State Fullerton and make it a full-time coaching job, it was a dream come true. I was even willing to take a big pay cut if I could get the job – luckily I got it and the pay was the same."

Garman, born March 27, 1944, compiled an overall record of 211 wins and 40 losses at Golden West (1972-79). At that time, quality softball facilities were nearly non-existent, especially at the junior college level, so Garman supervised the building of the softball facility (two lighted fields) at Golden West, which was considered one of the best complexes in southern California.

In July of 1979, however, Judi left the JC ranks to accept a full-time softball position at Cal State Fullerton as its first softball coach.

She quickly found, however, that work would also have to be done on the Cal Fullerton facilities. The 1980 field situation was described as a "three ring circus" with team home games on three different fields. She started at Cal Fullerton with next to nothing and encountered obstacles at nearly every corner. For example, her right fielder had to learn to play the sidewalk in front of her, the team's equipment was stored in a men's room, and keeping the pitching machine on required an extension cord thrown out the window of the carpentry shop. At Fullerton she led the efforts to get two lighted fields built on campus, and she and volunteers built a press box on the main field. They also assembled large sets of bleachers to complete the facility.

Judi had started a softball coaches' clinic while at Golden West (the first such clinic in the country) which grew from 35 attendees the first year to over 300 the following years. She also developed one-day player's clinics. According to Judi: "The toughest day was when 1200 athletes showed up and it rained. We had only one gym and used racket ball courts, removed the chairs in classrooms and used every overhang we could find. The result was that we were able to raise well over a million dollars to help fund the programs at Golden West and Fullerton. These funds helped buy bleachers, build press boxes, and buy extra gear."

Garman was also very successful at getting softball companies to sponsor the team (a new concept then) which provided much needed equipment as well as additional funds. The going statement among athletic sales people was, "Don't go asking Garman to buy your product – when you leave you will be paying them to use it."

She succeeded in building at Fullerton one of the top programs in the country, winning 50 games or more in eight consecutive seasons between 1981 and 1988 with 59 wins in 1987, 57 wins in 1986, and 56 wins in 1983. In 1986, her Cal State Fullerton Titans won the NCAA WCWS, defeating Texas A&M. In four earlier trips to the World Series, the Titans placed second twice and third twice. Judi Garman has a record of 913 wins 374 losses and 4 ties at Cal State Fullerton.

We asked Judi if she wouldn't mind providing a sense of those days before and around the beginning of Title IX. This is what she had to say in a piece she calls "The Way It Was":

"Before Title IX became fully entrenched and brought changes in philosophy along with increased job pressures, there was more camaraderie between teams and coaches. Examples:

"Fullerton and Texas A&M teams had a special relationship. The night before our national championship game (against each other) we went to a restaurant together. Parents joined us as well and the team players intermingled as we ate together. Teams also brought pictures of players as babies and we had to try and match players. The

next day we went out as competitors and played our hearts out. Players from both teams are still close friends after all these years!

"The PONY tournament at Fullerton was the premier college tournament. A special component was the 'talent show' the night before where each team performed. Who can forget Cal Poly's 'pillowcase people' and Cal Berkeley's parody of all the participating coaches? We would have a special motivational speaker as well (e.g., Olga Connolly and Pat McCormick). Then teams started saying they needed an extra game the night before the tournament or needed the time for some other purpose, so we lost this special night.

"I loved Bo Schembechler's philosophy of 'memory collecting.' When asked if he was going to allow his players to participate in all the festivities prior to the Rose Bowl game, he answered with a resounding 'yes.' He said that when players are talking to their grandkids years later it would be the "memories" they would be sharing.

"Whenever we traveled I would seek special experiences for our players. So our team, along with playing games, went camping in tents and once stayed in remote cabins in Sedona. We visited Sam Houston Maximum Security Prison and our 3rd baseman got an "A" in her criminal justice class after writing a report on our visit — we were also the last group permitted to visit as there was a hostage situation the following week. We traveled to Sweden and to Australia and New Zealand to play. We insisted on staying in private homes so we could experience their culture and when there we looked for unique things to do. This was different from most teams then, who stayed in hotels and worried about practice times. We had experiences in these countries that are 'memories of a lifetime.'

"We went to Hawaii regularly and also scheduled sightseeing when not playing. So we have been to the Polynesian Culture Center, snorkeled, sailed, and it was mandatory that each player go to Pearl Harbor at least once. I love getting letters and notes these days from former players thanking me for the travel experiences they had, and the accompanying memories.

"In 1986 I was invited to be the clinician for the first European Softball Clinic in Holland, Italy, and Czechoslovakia. It was an opportunity I did not want to give up even though it meant leaving my team for two weeks during preseason practice at the end of January. My thinking was I could leave my assistant coach to run practice; if things did not go well the team would really be happy I was back, and if things went well they would not even miss me. I had a great time and the team was ready for the season. We went 57-9 and won the National Championship. And I have great memories."

Doing Good by Being Good

As you have surmised already, one of Judi Garman's gifts is the ability to use her determination and creativity to fuel fundraising projects that enabled her to get around sources of negativity in institutions where she was employed. Judi refused to accept the traditional (at that time) role of the female athlete as second class citizen. She was steadfast in her commitment, consistent in her enthusiasm, and relentless in her determination. She would battle for what she believed was right and had no difficulty engaging in the noble fight.

Here, again in Judi's words, are her thoughts about the early struggles related to the passing of Title IX:

"The passing of Title IX gave us ground and clout for our demands for equality. It did not change attitudes and we always had to fight for our fair share. Never was anything automatically done. It was wearing and tiring to always have to fight an 'us' versus 'them' set of battles. From my perspective, I would work harder than my male counterparts and seldom got any benefits without a fight. AIAW was the leading organization fighting for what was right for women. Judith Holland, at UCLA, was a key fighter at this time and one I knew best. But the battles on the individual campuses were basically our own. Women AD's could only do so much.

"So battles fought were usually done on your own. The Women's Sports Organization took the leadership in fighting for Title IX implementation and in my later years we were able to get more generally-available information of how best to fight for equality. Sadly, each year I would ask my team what they knew about Title IX. As the years went by, fewer and fewer female softball players knew what it was."

Growing Smarter

Although born in Harrisburg, Pennsylvania, Judi moved with her family to Kindersley, Saskatchewan as a child and played softball and ran track. She recalled, "I didn't know at the time, but growing up where I did was probably the best thing that could have happened to me. Softball was the only sport available to me growing up in a small town on the Saskatchewan prairies. My mother loved softball and she would pitch to my sister and me so we could hit. We also played softball at Sunday school picnics and that is the first time I can remember playing a real game. In our small town we played all sports – following the seasons: football, hockey, baseball – but none were organized except boy's Little League. I started to play then and when we got to regionals I was kicked off the team for being a girl when the other teams objected. My coach fought for my right to play but was overruled.

"What we all loved was a game organized by the kids with no adults involved. The west side of town played the east side. We had our own tryouts, practices, built our own field (dug holes in the ground and called them dugouts). We had no uniforms but loved it. When the boys had to go to Little League because of their fathers, most hated it and some even quit – they liked our league better. We and the neighborhood kids played baseball from morning to night on the field we built. My sister and I were the only girls who played."

"My first chance to play organized ball was with Little League baseball. I was a pitcher and outfielder. I still remember at age 8, striking out my boyfriend. He started crying and I was almost traumatized. Then we traveled to play Eston in the play-offs. They would walk the batter in front of me to pitch to 'the girl.' I must have done okay, since the opposition then had me disqualified from playing any more games since I was not a boy."

"When my sister and I were in middle school, there was a women's softball team that invited us to join them. That was our start in organized softball. We would travel around to nearby towns and play at the town fairs. They would always have a soft-ball competition and we would play for prize money that would cover some of the expenses. Fields were terrible – just base paths cut out from the prairie grass, very rough, with chicken wire hung between old telephone poles for backstops. But I lived for the weekends when we would play. I loved the team aspect. It was so much more fun to play with friends than to play a solo sport."

"When I was a senior in high school in 1962 we moved to Saskatoon and there I saw an ad for tryouts for a women's team that was the top team in the city. I went to the first tryout and badly missed the ball on every swing. I had never seen such fast pitching. I went home and never even gave them my name. I thought I was so bad and I was so disappointed. The coach, how-ever, saw something in me and it took her several weeks to track me down and invite me to join their team. That was the Saska-toon Imperials and we went on to become Canadian Champions in 1969 and 1970 and represented Canada in the second ISF World Championships in Osaka, Japan."

Garman says winning those Canadian National Champi-onships (1969 and 1970) and competing in the World Champi-onship in Japan were the highlights of her career as a player. As a coach, the highlights were winning four consecutive national championships at Golden West College (1975-1978) and winning the Division I National Championship at Cal State Fullerton.

Although she retired from college coaching in 1999, Garman returned to coaching in 2000 as the head coach of the Italian National Team, leading it to the European Championship and fifth place in the 2000 ISF World Championship, which was held in her home town of Saskatoon.

Judi says it was her greatest event because she was returning to her home field in Saskatoon, "where my team had won the national championship in 1970. Having 7,000 fans stand and wave as the announcer welcomed home 'our own Judi Garman', it seemed my softball career had come full circle. I retired from coaching after that event."

Garman has written a "Softball Skills and Drills" book, published in 2001 by Human Kinetics. It is one of their top selling softball books and a rewritten second edition was just released in 2011.

In 1993, Garman was inducted into the National Fastpitch Coaches Hall of Fame and in 1995 was selected as the Learning for Life's Woman of the Year. In 2007, she was selected to the Cal State Fullerton Titan Hall of Fame. The Judi Garman Classic was renamed after her in 2006. The tournament was started in Garman's first year at Fullerton (1980) and was previously named the PONY and the KIA Classic. It is regarded as the premier midseason college softball tournament.

Judi isn't the only member of her family who has excelled in a sport. Her sister, Lorraine, is a member of the LPGA Hall of Fame, being inducted in 2009. She was the first women teaching professional to have her own teaching center and is recognized as an expert in club fitting. She is recognized as an LPGA Master Golf Professional and is one of the Golf Digest's top 20 women teachers.

Reflecting back on her career, Judi said that Gail Hopkins, manager and coach of the Saskatoon Imperials had the most influence on her career. "She taught me how to be organized and do whatever is necessary to give opportunities to your players and to get the job done, how to be positive and always believe in oneself. She took a group of players from a small city to the top of the Canadian softball world. We raised the money to travel 2,000 miles by train to Toronto to play our first National Championship. Trains went on strike and we had to ride the public bus home for the 2,000-mile return trip. Our first game was against the defending National Champion Toronto team and everyone felt sorry for our draw. We almost beat them. And the next year we were national champs!"

It is fortunate for USA college softball that its first full-time four-year-school coach had the determination and progressive approach to this new position. Her trailblazing set a standard and her good wishes for her sport have made it easy to enjoy her success. Judi Garman is that one-of-a-kind person who fit into the position that turned out to be ideally suited for her combination of charisma and caring.

After being highly successful at the JC level, Garman became the head coach at Cal State Fullerton in 1979 and compiled a record of 913-376 for a winning percentage of .708. (Photo courtesy Judi Garman)

Cindy Bristow speaks to a group of people who have attended one of the more than 30 to 40 clinics she gives each year through her company, Softball Excellence. (Photo courtesy of Cindy Bristow)

Chapter 19

CINDY BRISTOW
"MASTER EDUCATOR"

Growing Smarter

E very all-star team needs a person who is highly versatile, able to fill in many spots without a loss of that position's effectiveness or efficiency. From the time she began playing Major ball with the Lionettes, through her college career helping to recruit Carol Spanks at Cal Poly, up through becoming President of the National Coaches Association, National Director of Junior Olympic Softball for the ASA, Director of National Team and Coaching Development for the ASA, and Director of Development for the International Softball Federation, Cindy Bristow had the ability to make a difference wherever she turned her attention.

In addition, she has been a color analyst for ESPN softball coverage, author of eight softball instructional books, and has produced 14 instructional softball videos. And for good measure, she has worked with three different Olympic softball teams: USA, Greece, and China. Cindy Bristow is a member of the NFCA Softball Hall of Fame. In summary, she has been an amateur player, a professional player, a college coach, a professional coach, an administrator for the largest youth softball program in

Career Highlights
(Player, Coach, Program Developer)

- *President of the National Coaches Association*
- *National Director of Junior Olympics Softball for the ASA*
- *Director of National Teams and Coaching Development for USA Softball*
- *Director of Development for the ISF*
- *Coordinated the Greek Olympic Softball Team's creation and first-ever appearance in the Olympic Games*
- *Authored eight softball instructional books*
- *Produced 14 instructional videos on softball*
- *In 1981, won a gold medal as a member of the Sun City Saints in the Olympic Festival*
- *Board of Directors member, National Pro Fastpitch League*
- *Head Coach at Wichita State and New Mexico State*
- *Assistant Coach at Arizona State*
- *Head Coach and General Manager of the Georgia Pride, which later became the Florida Wahoos*
- *Named Coach of the Year leading Wahoos to league title*
- *Played on Cal Poly Pomona as co-player/coach with Barbara Reinalda, bringing it to a 3rd place finish in the AIAW National Championship*
- *Named All-Regional playing for Cal Poly Pomona*
- *In 1979, compiled a 19-2 pitching record, with 0.29 ERA, striking out a 137 batters in 143.2 innings.*
- *Played for the Orange Lionettes and Santa Ana Lionettes*

the United States, an administrator to help develop softball internationally, and currently the President of her own company, Softball Excellence, which can be easily found online. All told, Bristow has been involved in softball for over 35 years.

Growing up in Southern California, Cindy Bristow's father was a fan of the Orange Lionettes, one of the nation's top amateur teams which was founded in 1936 and lasted through 1976. He would come to Hart Park faithfully to watch the Lionettes, who won nine ASA national championships over four decades. Cindy said her dad, Whip, "lived and died for the Lionettes" and he passed the tradition on to his children. Bristow, who along with her sister Sue, played for the Lionettes from 1974-76, made the team at the age of sixteen.

While Bristow was growing up, the Riverside Parks and Recreation program didn't have a girl's program, so Cindy and her sister Sue appealed to Whip, who put together the Riverside Girls Softball League in 1970. "I learned from my parents that one of the most valuable things an athlete can learn is that you can do anything you put your mind to. I was always taught I could do anything I set my mind to and we were not allowed to say *can't* as kids."

So the seeds were planted early on for Bristow to overcome obstacles: watch for opportunities to learn, don't allow negativity to creep its way into your mindset, and put your flexibility and requisite variety to work. "There were times in the job as ASA JO Director that I was put into situations where, at first, I didn't have a clue in the world what to do. I just had to remember that you can do anything you set your mind to and work it out."

The Lionettes were supported by the community, which had a vested interest in the team. The Lionettes didn't have any big-time sponsors, so the players had to raise money for a trip to Japan when the team represented the ISF in the second Women's World Championship in Osaka, Japan. The players stood outside the markets in Orange, California and people gave them Blue Chip stamps. "And we redeemed them for $2 a book," said former Lionette Mickey Davis in a 1994 newspaper article in the Independent, "and before you know it, people were bringing us sacks of Blue Chip stamps."

Although Bristow only played in 20 games that first season for the Lionettes, she knew this was the place she wanted to be. "To me, this was the Yankees. It was women playing ball, the sport I loved." The Lionettes finished second in the PCWS League standings (15-9) and went 50-19 overall with Nancy Welborn (32-16) and Carol Spanks (18-3) as the top pitchers. In the 1975 Lionettes program, Bristow, now a senior in high school, was profiled with the following quote: "This youngster has a good attitude, works hard and has lots of ability. A fine asset to the Lionette organization." As a senior, Bristow received the Outstanding Senior Girl Athlete Award and the Kiwanis Award as the Outstanding Scholar Athlete. She was named MVP at LaSierra High School (Riverside) in softball and basketball.

Bristow says, however, "Softball picked me. I played all the other sports but not well. I hated running and couldn't jump very well, so that meant basketball, track and volleyball were out — and yet I loved sports. I always seemed good at the hand-eye coordination games and loved throwing a ball from as early as I can remember."

As a junior in high school, Bristow found out that she would have to dedicate herself to softball. "I made the Lionettes as a junior because they really wanted my sister (Sue), and felt bad cutting me — and I knew it. This was the first time in my life I was horrible and clueless about softball and hated that, so I dedicated myself in the off-season to changing that. I got up every morning at 5:30 and ran three miles with my brother Leon. Then I pitched 30 minutes, showered and went to school. I did this every day and by the next season it really showed. I was much better and actually had skills that could really contribute."

"Now keep in mind that I was playing with the likes of Carol Spanks, Shirley Topley, Mickey Davis, and Joan Joyce, so I was clearly out of my league, but this greater talent influence was a game changer for me. It taught me that there is always room to improve and the sport is way bigger than any of its participants." Because of her dedication and devotion to softball, Bristow admits, "I really never had a social life growing up outside of softball since I was always practicing, going to practice, or playing softball somewhere. It didn't seem like a sacrifice, since I loved it and only wanted to hang out with other softball players. They seemed more dedicated than the people I was going to high school with."

Here we have an echo of Carol Spanks' thoughts about the benefits of ASA camaraderie among teammates whose age could vary by as much as twenty years or more. Compared to dedicated athletes caught up in a goal to win or place well in a National Championship, the day-to-day events of senior high school life seemed a little dull. Compare this to Cat Osterman's feelings of burn-out when she returned from the adrenalin-crushing excitement of being on an Olympic gold medal team for nearly a year and then going back to your college team for fall ball. It takes some adjusting.

Bristow had to appeal to the NCAA to play college softball (she was classified a pro). "They let us play, me only three years, but Sue was allowed to play all four. The first year our softball coach was also the women's basketball coach. She actually missed our first National Tournament with a bad back. So both Barb Reinalda and I were the coaches since we were also pitchers. We went to the National championship in Omaha, Nebraska without a coach and finished third. That would never happen now."

At the conclusion of the season when the basketball coach decided to coach the single sport, there was an opening in softball. Bristow and her delegation went to Carol Spanks to ask her to fill it. After joining the Cal Poly Pomona team, Spanks worked out a plan with Shirley Topley so that Spanks would be head coach of the college team with Topley serving as assistant, and in the summer Topley would be head coach of the Lionettes and Spanks would serve as assistant.

The result for Bristow was tremendous. "I will never forget Spanks and Topley sitting us down and telling us, 'You represent your family, your team, your sport, and female athletes, so make sure that anyone who sees you do anything, whether you know it or not, leaves with a great impression.' I've never forgotten that and always tried to represent each of these factors in my life with pride."

Doing Good by Being Good

At some point in college, while coaching a high school basketball team, Cindy Bristow realized that softball was in her future. "From everything I knew about softball through the Lionettes and Cal Poly, if I didn't coach softball it would be a crime. That's when I decided to go to Arizona State University and see if I could be an assistant coach there to Mary Littlewood."

As Littlewood's assistant Bristow learned loyalty and humility. "I learned from Mary when she sat a cocky assistant – me – down and told me that my job was to support her, period. That I was only coaching by her choice and she could change that choice at any moment. Best coaching lesson I ever learned and I still thank her for that to this day. And be classy in everything you do, which I learned from Carol Spanks. She's absolutely the best and I was blessed, privileged and honored to have played with and for her."

In addition to the people mentioned above, Bristow's parents had an important influence on their daughter's softball career. "They both encouraged me and my sister to play. They were both excellent softball players and they practiced with us, coached us, told us to work harder if we weren't happy with playing time, and kept us grounded by reminding us to always consider our two brothers and sister who weren't getting these same choices in case we ever felt too big for our britches."

After moving from the assistant's job at ASU to a year at New Mexico state and two years as head coach at Wichita State, Cindy was selected in 1987 from more than 100 candidates to become the first director of the ASA Junior Olympic Program. Before Bristow's full-time position, the program had a beginning but it didn't have either direction or focus.

Grace Under Pressure

Bristow had this to say about the position: "I saw the opportunity to influence coaches at the grassroots level so they could start to correctly teach young athletes how to play the game properly. At the college level, I was seeing the other side of the spectrum, where great natural athletes were very frustrated because they had not been properly taught the fundamentals."

Bristow began with a collegial approach to this educational problem and opportunity. Bobby Simpson, ASA commissioner in Georgia, was particularly helpful. He worked with her to establish the JO program, to learn how the ASA operates with its network of local associations throughout the United States. In time this effort reaped benefits, particularly in the area of coaches' education. "One of the major things we've done is become one of the leaders in the sport related to coaches' education," said Bristow. "When I got here, ASA was the leader of softball, but as far as some of the specific areas, we had some growing to do. Now we have a complete library of resources available to the coaches in our program and to the administrators at the local level." Bristow established the VIP program for coaches with three levels: gold, silver and bronze, which helped propel the registration of coaches in the program and create interest in children playing JO softball.

Bristow also played a role, along with Marita Hynes, former OU administrator, in bringing the Women's College World Series to Oklahoma City, Oklahoma. The early days in Oklahoma City were tough. Once Oklahoma City got the Women's College World Series, Bristow, Hynes and everyone involved found out there was nothing easy about running the event and getting people to volunteer – particularly in the parking lot.

With the event being new, attendance was down. "Crowds were still school supportive instead of being softball supportive. Unless OU or OSU made it, we were toast as far as crowds were concerned. Marita and I would just pray that either OU or OSU would win Regionals and get to the World Series. Remember this was back before the Super Regionals and before softball was on TV or in the Olympics."

Bristow and Hynes both ran the first coaches meeting. "Marita would do the technical stuff and then I'd go over the tornado evacuation plan. I can still remember Sharron Backus at our first coaches' meeting. That was the first time UCLA had ever played in Oklahoma, so I'm going over the whole 'go down to the bottom of the stadium, into the interview room and you'll be fine.' Sharron's eyes were as big as basketballs and I tell her, 'It's not like the Wizard of Oz, that's just a movie.' Marita always made me do that part of the meeting because all of these teams were petrified of tornadoes since none of them had played much, if at all, in Oklahoma."

"At the time we started hosting the WCWS, we had the only softball stadium in the country. I can remember Mike Candrea walking around with me and asking a lot of questions and looking at everything, because he'd just gotten the funding to build his own stadium and he used the Hall of Fame Stadium as his model." Bristow said that having the stadium was the one reason they got and were able to keep the WCWS in Oklahoma City. "It was the blueprint on which every single softball stadium in the U.S. has been built," said Cindy. "It was ground zero for softball stadiums, so we can thank [former ASA Executive Director] Don Porter and his vision."

The media who attended in those early days was small compared to who attends now. "Back then our interview/pressroom was down in the basement of the stadium. It was dark and dingy and small. But when you don't have much media attending, it's perfect."

Bristow is amazed now at how big the event has grown. "I'd never gone back since the last event Marita and I ran together until a few years ago, and it's still unbelievable to me. The additional seating, new scoreboard, extra tents, facility upgrades, and crowds are just amazing. I could still see a glimmer of the old tournament in its current-day version, but just barely."

There is another way that Cindy Bristow showed grace under pressure. This particular time involved coming to the rescue of Bobby Simpson when he was in charge of an ASA National Coaching School event and the speaker became ill. According to Simpson, "I was really glad that Cindy Bristow was there even though she was not supposed to be. It was the mid-1980's and Cindy called to say that she would pinch instruct. All I really knew was that she coached at Wichita State. However, I sensed on the phone that she was passionate and would do a good job. I was wrong about her doing a good job – she did a phenomenal job. Needless to say, I asked her to help at many more clinics and she was absolutely terrific. She was knowledgeable, yet eager to learn. She related well to everybody from veteran coaches to beginning players. She was mentally tough, yet compassionately tender. She was dependable, consistent, flexible, and

I knew she would climb extremely high on the softball ladder. I also know that she will never lose her solid connection to her roots and her cap size would not change as acclaim came her way."

Simpson continues, "After sharing many experiences with Cindy, I am convinced that her most important impact has been on the individuals that she spent time with. It might be Anna, a dedicated 27-year old Greek lady wanting to learn to pitch so she could represent her country in the Olympics. It could be Kayla, a skilled athlete taking lessons in Tampa in an effort to play college softball. Maybe it was an 8-year old in Alaska, or a veteran coach needing some help, or a summer at a clinic sharing a conversation in the hall, or even someone at the top of the game's hierarchy as a player or administrator. Cindy Bristow always has time, always cares and is patiently seeking to help that person while caring very little who gets the credit for the improvement.

"Cindy is extremely dynamic, solidly confident and yet never arrogant. Today she has risen to the point where she is often on center stage and she is excellent in that location. However, I proclaim that she is even better in the small, unseen, relatively quiet conversations that she conducts with the Anna's and Kayla's. She is the ultimate giver."

Cindy Bristow shows an aspiring player how to properly catch the softball. (Photo courtesy Cindy Bristow)

Cindy Bristow (above) demonstrates a pitching mechanic at a clinic and (below) shows the batter how to properly shift her weight in hitting. (Photos courtesy of Cindy Bristow)

Gathering for a reunion of the Pacific Coast Women's Softball League (PCWSL) in 1990 at Cal Poly Pomona were these members of the ASA National Softball Hall of Fame. Kneeling (from left) Billie Harris, Jeanne Contel, Carol Spanks, Dot Wilkinson and Ricki Caito. Middle row (from left) Sharron Backus, Margaret Dobson, Sis King, Rosie Adams, and Ruth Sears. Back row (from left) Jackie Rice, Nancy Welborn, E. Louise Albrecht, Mickey Davis, Shirley Topley, Bertha Tickey, Gloria May and Margie Law. These players represented some of the best teams in amateur softball including the Raybestos Brakettes, the Fresno Rockets, the Orange Lionettes, the Erv Lind Florists and the Phoenix Ramblers.

THE 20TH
"BEST OF THE BEST"

In Chapter One, I described how the 19 "Best of the Best" were selected, and asked you, the reader, to engage in a similar exercise either alone or with other softball players and fans. If you did that, my guess is that you would find that the top 10 or so are easy, but after that the list becomes a bit fuzzy as different eras and comparisons are more subjective than objective.

Throughout the writing and researching of this book, Steve has asked me to keep a record of whatever names might pop up as worthy of "top 20" attention – which is why the list includes only 19. I have put together that list, which contains players and coaches who could easily be included alongside the 19 I selected. They are listed in alphabetic order, along with a top career accomplishment or two to demonstrate that we clearly know how great each and everyone in this chapter has been to the enjoyment and development of our game.

To each of you listed here, let me salute you for being in the group of people who I think of as outstanding difference makers.

•**Leah O'Brien-Amico**, outfielder, first base, pitcher, named to NCAA 25th anniversary team, .428 career batting average at Arizona, three-time all-tourney WCWS, member of ASA National Softball Hall of Fame, member of 1996, 2000 and 2004 Olympic teams.

•**Kathy Arendsen**, 337-26 record for Raybestos Brakettes, nine national titles, pitched Texas Women's University to 1979 title; two-time AIAW All-American, former college coach, and now director of volunteer development at United Way of Lane County in Springfield, OR.

•**Laura Berg**, outfielder, four-time All-American at Fresno State, member of four Olympic teams, member of NCAA 25th anniversary team, had 396 hits in career, second all-time in NCAA, named to 1998 all-tournament team of WCWS, compiled .414 career batting average.

•**Courtney Blades**, pitcher Southern Miss, compiled 151-34 record, pitched perfect game against Arizona in 2000 WCWS, named all-tournament WCWS in 2000, averaged 9.8 strikeouts per game in college, 1,773 in 1,261.2 innings, 1997-2000, 5th all-time.

•**Gayle Blevins**, former head coach at Iowa and Indiana University, (1980-87), retired from Iowa in 2010, compiled overall record of 1,245-588-5 for .679 winning percentage, was 945-440-3 at Iowa (1988-2010), led Hawkeyes to four appearances in WCWS, led Indiana to three WCWS, won 5 Big Ten titles.

•**Leah Braatz**, catcher, first four-time All-American in Arizona history, slugged 85 homers, and drove in 322 runs in college with .797 slugging percentage, compiled .381 career batting average and .966 fielding percentage, in 1997 made only three errors in 353 chances for a .992 fielding percentage, named to 25th NCAA anniversary team.

•**Suzy Brazney**, catcher, third base, played from 1980-2005, named to a record 20 ASA All-America teams, member of six Olympic Festival teams, member of three USA Pan Am teams, winning gold medals in 1987 and 1991, member of 1990 USA ISF World Championship team, Canada Cup gives award each year in her honor to top catcher, member of Cal Poly Pomona Hall of Fame and ASA National Softball Hall of Fame.

•**Bob Brock**, head coach Sam Houston State, former head coach at Texas A&M, in five WCWS, won two titles,1983 and 1987, finished runner-up twice, 1986 and 1984, and fifth in 1988 for 18-8 record, overall record is 981-588-1, won AIAW national title in 1982 at Texas A&M.

•**Crystl Bustos**, shortstop, third base, member of three USA Olympic teams, 2000, 2004 and 2008, batted .500 with six homers and 10 RBI in 2008 Olympics, was Pan American Games gold medalist in 2007, member of 2006 ISF World Championship team, batted .500, batted .346 in 2004 Olympics, two-time NJCAA All-American and two-time NJCAA Player of Year, named MVP in pro softball league in 1998.

•**Joyce Compton**, former head coach South Carolina and Missouri, compiled 951-486-3 record at South Carolina, 1987-2010, and 115-77 record at Missouri, 1983-86, former first baseman for the Connecticut Falcons of the pro league, played for Raybestos Brakettes, 1973-75, compiled .338 batting average with 142 RBI.

•**Tracy Compton**, pitcher, UCLA, combined with Debbie Doom for perfect game in WCWS, 5-29-1982, named all-tourney WCWS 1985, compiled 72-10 record with career ERA, 0.15, lowest in NCAA history, member of UCLA Athletic Hall of Fame, compiled 56-4 record with the Raybestos Brakettes.

•**Sheila Cornell Douty**, first baseman, DH, member of 1996 and 2000 USA Olympic teams, starred in college at UCLA, member of ASA and ISF Halls of Fame, played for Los Angeles Blazers/Diamonds and Raybestos Brakettes, 16-time ASA All-American, member of seven national championship teams and three runners-up, member of four USA Pan American teams.

•**Pat Dufficy**, infielder-outfielder, Raybestos Brakettes, 1977-83, 85-95, 97, Raybestos leader in seven categories, twice member of USA Pan American team, member of ASA Hall of Fame, 11-time ASA All-American at three positions, member of 10 ASA national championship teams, played in 11 U.S. Olympic Festivals, member three ISF World Championship teams.

•**Jo Evans**, coach, Texas A&M, former coach at Colorado State, and Utah, compiled 26-year record of 902-496-2 for a .645 winning percentage.

•**Nancy Evans**, pitcher, Arizona, compiled 120-8 record for .938 percentage, best in NCAA history, former assistant coach at Arizona, 1998-2007, MOP of 1997 WCWS, member of three NCAA championship teams, now assistant coach at DePaul.

•**Laura Espinoza**, shortstop, had .766 slugging percentage at Arizona, drove in 315 runs and hit 85 home runs, now a high school coach in Arizona (Empire High), twice led NCAA in homers, 1994 and 1995, and runs batted in, had 1.004 slugging percentage in 1995 to lead nation.

•**Sandy Fischer**, former head coach Oklahoma State, former pro player for Connecticut Falcons, compiled record of 883-358-3 in 23 years, coached Michele Smith.

•**Bill Galloway**, former head coach Texas A&M and Louisiana Tech, compiled record of 881-390-2 for .693 winning percentage.

•**Patty Gasso**, head coach, Oklahoma, won 2000 NCAA WCWS, has compiled overall record of 979-328-2 and is 811-

269-2 at OU, led teams to five WCWS appearances, Winningest coach in Big 12 history.

•**Suzie Gaw**, shortstop, outfield, 11-time ASA All-American, member of four USA Pan Am teams, played in eight U.S. Olympic Festivals, member of ASA Hall of Fame and Arizona Softball Foundation Hall of Fame.

•**Yvette Girouard**, former head coach LSU, 526-171-1 record, retired after 2011 season with 1,285-421-1 overall record and .753 winning percentage, one of only three coaches to lead two programs to WCWS, 2005 NFCA Hall of Fame inductee, coached at Louisiana-Lafayette from 1981-2000.

•**Dr. Joanne Graf**, Florida State, coached from 1979-2008 at Florida State, won two AIAW slow pitch titles before switching to fast pitch, compiled overall record of 1,437-478-6 and was 1,218-425-6 in NCAA Division One, teams made seven trips to WCWS and won 10 Atlantic Coast titles, 21 NCAA regional appearances.

•**Keira Goerl**, pitcher, compiled 130-21 record at UCLA, (2001-04), including pitching no-hitter in 2003 WCWS championship game, M0P of 2003 WCWS, one of three pitchers to be winning pitcher in two WCWS championship games (2003-04).

•**Michele Granger**, southpaw pitcher, former University of California four-time All-American, compiled 119-52 record, pitched opening game of 1996 Olympics, only player in history to play in Pan American Games, ASA Women's Major, U.S. Olympic Festival and Junior Girls World in same season (1987), member of ASA and ISF Halls of Fame, now coaches youth softball.

•**Alicia Hollowell**, pitcher, Arizona, named MOP in 2006 WCWS, fanned 1,768 batters in career, sixth all-time, compiled 144-23 record with .862 winning percentage, two-time all-tourney WCWS selection (2003 and 2006).

•**Carol Hutchings**, head coach, Michigan, won 2005 NCAA WCWS, compiled overall record of 1,209 wins and 479 losses, in 2005 helped select both the USA Softball National and Elite teams and was appointed head coach for the Elite team at the Canada Cup and was assistant coach for the National Team at the Japan Cup.

•**Lisa Ishikawa**, pitcher, starred at Northwestern compiling 97-30 record with 0.47 ERA, 1,200 strikeouts in 914.1. innings, pitched for Raybestos Brakettes, 1985-1986, Big Ten Freshman of Year, 1985 ASA Sportswoman of the Year, two-time Big Ten MVP, hurled 14 no-hitters, winner of Southland Olympia Award, 1985, led Northwestern to three WCWS appearances.

•**Nancy Ito**, former catcher for the Orange Lionettes, 13-time ASA All-American, member of four national championship teams and four runners-up, died in 1987, member of ASA National Softball Hall of Fame.

•**Margo Jonker**, head coach Central Michigan, compiled record of 1,037-620-5 from 1980-2011, former assistant coach for 2000 USA Olympic Team, member of four Halls of Fame, including NFCA, former assistant coach for 1999 USA Pan American team.

•**Diane Kalliam**, outfield, played 15 years and compiled .427 lifetime batting average, twice led ASA National Championship in batting, 1974 (.444) and 1975 (.632), played in seven ASA national championships and batted .430, was named ASA All-American five times, member of ASA National Softball Hall of Fame, after amateur career, played pro softball and batted .379 in 1976 to finish second in the league in batting, member of San Mateo Hall of Fame (1994) and Cal State Hayward (1986), coached at San Francisco State University from 1979-99.

•**Danielle Lawrie**, led Washington to NCAA national title, 2009, hurled no-hitter against DePaul in 2007 WCWS, named MOP of 2009 WCWS, 4th all-time in strikeouts, 1,860, compiled 136-41 record in college, member of Canadian Olympic team, 2008, two-time NCAA Player of Year, 2009-2010.

•**Eugene Lenti**, head coach DePaul, has compiled record of 1,102 wins, 527 losses and six ties for a .676 winning percentage.

•**Lisa Longaker**, pitcher, member of NCAA 25th anniversary team, compiled 89-12 record at UCLA, was member of three national championship teams (1988-1990), three-time WCWS all-tournament selection, (1987, 1988 and 1990), pitched 1988 national championship game beating Fresno State, 3-0.

•**Donna Lopiano**, pitcher, infielder, starred for the Raybestos Brakettes for 10 years, compiling 183-18 record with 1,633 strikeouts, named ASA All-American eight times, former athletic director at University of Texas, former CEO of the Women's Sports Foundation, had 281 RBI in 10 years.

•**Jessica Mendoza**, outfielder, four-time All-American at Stanford, member of 2004 and 2008 USA Olympic team, made pro debut in 2005, was second in batting in pro league in 2011 (.379). named to all-tourney in WCWS in 2001, led NCAA in batting in 2000 with .475 average.

•**Jay Miller**, former USA National Team coach, has compiled record of 1,004-688 for a .600 winning percentage, former coach at Missouri, Mississippi State and Oklahoma City University.

•**Tayrne Mowatt**, pitcher, outfielder, Arizona, named MOP of 2007 WCWS, compiled 100-33 record in college, senior year won ESPY and Best Female College Athlete, two-time all-tourney WCWS pick, member of ASA national champion in 2005.

•**Clint Myers**, head coach Arizona State, won two NCAA WCWS, 2008 and 2011, overall coaching record is 805-120 (.870 winning percentage) and is 324-79 at ASU, (.804 winning percentage), led teams to five WCWS in six years.

•**Debbie Nichols**, Louisiana Tech, pitcher, compiled 149-45 record, 1987-90, for .768 winning percentage in 198 games and 1,373 innings. Hurled 84 shutouts.

•**Diane Ninemire**, head coach California, won 2002 NCAA WCWS, has compiled record of 1,059 wins and 509 losses for a .675 winning percentage.

•**Susie Parra**, pitcher, Arizona, former member of USA National Team, compiled 101-9 record at Arizona (1991-1994) for .918 winning percentage, third best all-time, member of two NCAA national championship teams, pitching 1993 championship game, beating UCLA, 1-0, and 1994 championship, beating Cal State Northridge, 4-0.

•**Marilyn Rau**, catcher, 11-time ASA All-American, member of 1979 ASA National Champion, named tourney MVP in 1979, member of 1979 Pan Am team, member of 1978 USA National Team, in 1979 named Arizona's Athlete of Year, member of ASA Hall of Fame and Arizona Softball Foundation Hall of Fame.

•**Barbara Reinalda**, compiled 441-31 pitching record during 19-year career with Brakettes, recorded 2,172 strikeouts, had 45-6 record in ASA national championship play, hurled 19 perfect games and 31 no-hitters, 76 one-hitters, 312 shutouts, 11-time ASA All-American, now head coach at Yale University.

•**Kay Rich**, member of ASA Hall of Fame, could play just about any position on softball diamond, batted .400 or higher three times in ASA national championship play, batted .611 with 10 RBI in 1955 national tourney, batted .371 in eight nationals between 1949-1957, named MVP in 1954 ASA national tourney, batted .444 in 1949 ASA national when pitching distance was 38 feet, named ASA All-American eight times.

•**Marge Ricker**, former coach Orlando Rebels, 1954-1985, compiled record of 1,470 wins and 476 losses for .760 winning percentage, teams competed in 26 ASA nationals and finished fifth or higher 22 times, won 1981 ASA Women's Major Fast Pitch title, three of her former players are members of ASA Hall of Fame including Dot Richardson, originator of the Rebel Games, led USA team to a fourth place in 1982 ISF World Championship, member of ASA Hall of Fame.

•**Diane Schumacher**, first base, pitcher, in 1993 first American to be inducted into ISF Hall of Fame, seven-time ASA All-American, compiled .329 lifetime batting average, played for Raybestos Brakettes from 1976-1986, led team in batting five times, twice a member of the USA Pan Am team.

•**Amanda Scott**, four-time All-American at Fresno State, named to NCAA 25th anniversary team, compiled 106-18 record, twice lead nation in ERA, 1999 and 2000, MOP of 1998 WCWS, hurled no-hitter in 1998 WCWS against Michigan, 8-0.

•**Julie Smith**, second base, starred at Texas A&M and Fresno State, member of 1996 Olympic team, member of 1987 USA Junior National team, named to NCAA's women's College World Series All Decade Team in 1991, Fresno State Athlete of the Year, 1990-1991, member of four ASA national championship teams.

•**Elaine Sortino**, Massachusetts, has compiled record of 1,129 wins, 470 losses and six ties for a .705 winning percentage, 2004 inductee into NFCA Hall of Fame, eighth coach to win 1,000 games, first coach in NE to collect 700 wins.

•**Bertha Tickey**, pitcher, pitched for Orange Lionettes and Raybestos Brakettes, member of ASA National Softball Hall of Fame, Connecticut ASA Hall of Fame and Orange County Hall of Fame, compiled record of 757 wins and 88 losses with 162 no-hitters, member of 11 ASA national championship teams.

•**Angela Tincher**, former Virginia Tech pitcher, 2005-2008, one of only three pitchers to have 2,000 or more strikeouts in college career,

(2,149), in 2008 led NCAA in strikeouts (651) and ERA (0.63), 2008 USA Player of the Year and named to WCWS all-tourney team.

•**Shirley Topley**, first baseman, manager, starred for Orange Lionettes, 11-time ASA All-American, led Orange County Majestics to ASA national title in 1987, was assistant coach for USA 1995 and 1999 Pan American teams, assistant coach for 2000 Olympic team and 1990 USA National Team for ISF World Championship, member ASA National Softball Hall of Fame.

•**Ralph Weekly, Karen Weekly**, co-head coaches Tennessee, Ralph has compiled record of 1,015 wins, 343 losses and two ties, former assistant coach of 1996 USA Olympic softball team, led team to one second and two third places in WCWS. Karen has 737-259-2 overall record at UT and Chattanooga.

•**Linda Wells**, former head coach Minnesota and Arizona State, assistant coach of 1987 USA Pan American team, former fast pitch player, compiled coaching record of 914-679-1.

•**Rhonda Wheatley**, pitcher, Cal Poly Pomona, 1984-1987, hurled longest game in NCAA WCWS, 25 innings against Texas A&M in 1984, losing 1-0, compiled 139-60 record with 83 shutouts in college with 0.40 ERA, member of 1987 USA Pan American team.

•**Teresa Wilson**, compiled record of 839-526-1, former head coach at Washington and Texas Tech, former Arizona assistant coach, led Washington to six NCAA WCWS including finals twice and semi-finals twice, assistant coach of 1998 USA National Team, which won ISF World championship, compiled 532-198-1 record at Washington.

•**Dot Wilkinson**, outstanding catcher, named ASA All-American 19 times during her career, 1933 to 1965. Member of three national championship teams, also an outstanding bowler who is a member of International Bowling Hall of Fame, inducted into ASA Hall of Fame in 1970…named Arizona's eighth best all time athlete in 1999, born Oct. 9, 1921.

ACKNOWLEDGEMENTS

Bill and Steve are grateful for the contributions of many people in the preparation and planning of this book. First, we are reminded of our original connection, which occurred while writing and preparing *Ty Stofflet: Softball's Lefty Legend*. It was Ty Stofflet who understood that we had a lot in common and could work well together. Eight years later, that idea continues to hold true. Thanks, Ty. We also benefited from a conversation Steve had with New Jersey ASA Commissioner Leo Spirito and his wife Patricia. The conversation reminded Steve that there might be an interesting book project where he and Bill could again collaborate. The result of that collaboration is the *Best of the Best*.

Bill is particularly grateful for the contributions that the following people made in the preparation of research material used as background for the *Best of the Best*: Marita Hynes, O.W. "Bill" Smith, Connie Claussen, Beth Richards, and Mary Littlewood each added insights and information regarding the history of women's fast pitch softball. Marita's focus was on the history of the Women's College World Series in Oklahoma City. Bill added material on the Women's College World Series events in Omaha, Nebraska. Connie supplied Omaha event information, as well. Beth included background information about the beginnings of the World Series. Mary Littlewood was very helpful in describing what it was like to coach women's fast pitch softball in the 1960s and 1970s.

Stormy Irwin provided photos of Sharron Backus and Carol

Spanks. Debbie Darrah at the Texas A & M Sports Information Department went to extra lengths to research background information on Shawn Andaya. James Ybiernas at the UCLA Sports Information Department was a great source of facts and statistics of former UCLA players who were profiled in the book along with providing outstanding photos of these former Bruins.

Julie Bartel at the Communications Department for USA Softball was particularly supportive of this project from the moment it was discussed. The USA Team photos came directly from her department with speed, thoroughness, and accuracy. She also made it easy to conduct essential research. We are grateful for her support.

Robin L. Pokoj of Softball Excellence, was quick and effective in providing various photos of Cindy Bristow. Mike Noteware, Oklahoma State University, also provided essential help by adding Michele Smith's college picture to the book.

Katrina McCormack at the Sports Information Department of Florida Atlantic University provided photos and background information on Joan Joyce. Mike Carmo provided the photo of Team Watley after the team won the ASA 10-and-under National Championship in 2011.

Bob Brock, head softball coach at Sam Houston State University, was a tremendous help in providing background information and insight about Shawn Andaya, one of his former players when he coached at Texas A & M. Ralph Weekly, head softball coach at University of Tennessee, provided similar assistance in the preparation of background information for Monica Abbott.

Bobby Simpson, owner of Higher Ground in Tifton, Georgia, was particularly helpful in providing background information for the Cindy Bristow profile.

Steve, back East, would also like to thank the following people for helping the book project make progress during its various stages from idea through completed book:

First, Bill Miller was an essential partner through all phases of the project. His dedication and faith in the book kept it moving in the right direction. Bill also brought his love of the women's game to all project considerations. Without his support, it is not clear there would have been a book. There certainly would not have been this particular book.

Mike Krupa has once again managed all changes in the manuscript with his typically high levels of grace and charm. There are many value-adds that he made part of the finished product. Mike's levels of cooperation and goodwill make him a terrific publishing partner and we are pleased to have his experience and competence as part of our team.

A special salute to Adam Kaufman for the many times he turned unsolvable computer problems into workable solutions.

My older son, Joseph Dougherty, provided many valuable contributions to the shape of this project. We are grateful for his interest and effort in making the book much better than it might have been and for his steadfast uncompromising focus on quality. My younger son, David Clarfield, proved yet again that he has acquired the editorial skills to make a book better than the authors believed it could be. Thank you, David, for being thorough and working with dispatch.

Rocky Leavelle was very helpful in identifying ways to improve the structure of the text. Robin Clarfield Tolvin, my sister, has once again lent a strong measure of support and encouragement to this project. I value her thoughts and enjoy her ideas

Patricia, my wife, is a seasoned partner in these projects who makes sure that there will be family Quality of Life during the *sturm und drang* in the lifetime of a book reaching print.

Thank you all.

ABBREVIATIONS

AAU-Amateur Athletic Union. Is one of the largest non-profit volunteer sports organizations in the United States. A multi-sport organization, the AAU is dedicated exclusively to the promotion and development of amateur sports and physical fitness programs.

AIAW-Association for Intercollegiate Athletics for Women. Was founded in 1971 to govern collegiate women's athletics in the United States and to administer national championships. It evolved out of the Commission on Intercollegiate Athletics for Women (founded in 1967). The association was one of the biggest advancements for women's athletics on the collegiate level.

ASA-Amateur Softball Association. Is the national governing body of softball in the United States with its headquarters located in Oklahoma City The ASA has 76 local associations nationwide that register teams and umpires and promote and develop softball.

ERA-Earned Run Average. In softball statistics, ERA is the mean of earned runs given up by a pitcher per seven innings pitched.

ESPN-Entertainment and Sports Programming Network. Is an American global television network focusing on sports-related programming—including live and taped event telecasts, sports talk shows, and other original programming.

ISF-International Softball Federation. Is the international governing body for softball throughout the world with its headquarters located in Plant City, Fla.

MOP-Most Outstanding Player. Each year at the NCAA Women's College World Series, an award is given to the Most Outstanding Player in the WCWS.

MVP-Most Valuable Player. Is an award typically given to the best performing player or players on a specific team, an entire league or for a particular contest or a series of contests.

NCAA-National Collegiate Athletic Association. Is a semivoluntary association of 1,281 institutions, conferences, organizations and individuals that organizes the athletic programs of many colleges and universities in the United States.

NFCA-National Fastpitch Coaches Association. Is the professional growth organization for fastpitch softball coaches from all competitive levels of play with a membership of more than 4,500.

NJCAA-National Junior College Athletic Association. Founded in 1938, the National Junior College Athletic Association is an association of community college and junior college athletic departments throughout the United States.

NPF-National Pro Fastpitch. Formerly the Women's Pro Softball League (WPSL), is the only professional women's softball league in the United States.

PCWSL-Pacific Coast Women's Softball League. Was originally one of the best women's fast pitch softball leagues in the United States and was founded in 1946 as the Western States Girls Softball League by Ford Hoffman, Erv Lind, Dennis Murphy and Shorty Hill. It was later renamed in 1951.

UCLA-University of California at Los Angeles. Is a public research university located in the Westwood neighborhood of Los Angeles, California.

USOC-United States Olympic Committee. Is a non-profit organization that serves as the National Olympic Committee (NOC)for the United States and coordinates the relationship between the United States.

USSSA-United States Specialty Sports Association. Is a volunteer, sports body, non-profit organization based in Kissimmee, Florida. It was founded in 1968, originally in Petersburg, Virginia, and registered slow pitch softball teams, but in 1998 expanded to include other sports. It has a membership of more than 3.7 million involved in 13 sports.

WCWS-Women's College World Series. The name of the event where the top eight women's college softball teams compete in Oklahoma City to decide the national champion. Except for 1996, the event has been held in Oklahoma City every year since 1990

END NOTES

Overview of end notes: End notes reflect two fundamental sources: (1) Direct communication between the athletes, coaches and Bill Plummer. All of the quotations and information were acquired between March and August, 2011. These quotes and information will not be given separate citations. (2) Information from other sources. Any information from a source other than the two authors will be cited specifically as will be the source of all career highlights. Citations are made for any information and quotation taken from sources other than Bill Plummer's interviews. All Plummer's interviews occurred between March and August, 2011, with the athletes and coaches.

•Introduction: Keltner, D. (2009) *Born to be good: The science of a meaningful life*. New York: W.W. Norton & Company. W. Ross Ashby, *An Introduction to Cybernetics*. London: Methuen & Co. Ltd. 1964. Law of Requisite Variety pg. 206. Tieg quotation used in his professional programs, as told by Gerald Kass, O. D. to Dr. Clarfield.

•Lisa Fernandez: "In the Zone: The World's Best Female Softball Player" by Michele Kort, *Los Angeles Weekly*, April 2-9, 1993. Career statistics were compiled from Lisa Fernandez website, www.LisaFernandez.com. NCAA Softball Records Book and USA Softball Olympic Team Guides.

•Michele Smith: Career statistics were compiled from the Michele Smith website, www.MicheleSmith.com NCAA Softball Records Book and USA Softball Olympic Team Guides.

•Cat Osterman: Osterman's career highlights were compiled from the University of Texas website, NCAA Softball Records Book and USA Softball Olympic Team Guides.

•Natasha Watley: Natasha Watley's career statistics were compiled from UCLA website, NCAA Softball Records Book and USA Softball Olympic Team Guides.

•Stacey Nuveman: David Leon Moore, "Nuveman carries a lot of clout," USA TODAY, 22 April 2002. Stacey Nuveman's career highlights were compiled from the UCLA website, NCAA Softball

Records Book, USA Softball Olympic Team Guides and Stacey Nuveman's website.

•Jennie Finch: "Jennie Finch closes out career with Team USA as champion," USA Today, 26 July 2010 www.finchwindmill.com. Jennie Finch's career highlights were compiled from the Arizona website, NCAA Softball Records Book, and USA Softball Olympic Team Guides.

•Moncia Abbott: Monica Abbott's career highlights were compiled from the University of Tennessee website, NCAA Softball Records Book and USA Softball Olympic Team Guides.

•Dot Richardson: Dot Richardson's career highlights were compiled from Dot's website, www.dotrichardson.com, the NCAA Records Book and USA Softball Olympic Team Guides.

•Shawn Andaya: Shawn Andaya's career highlights were compiled from the Texas A&M website, newspaper articles furnished, and the 2007 NCAA College World Series Records Book, 1982-2006.

•Debbie Doom: Debbie Doom's career highlights were compiled from the UCLA website, the NCAA Softball Records Book and the 2007 NCAA College World Series Records Book, 1982-2006.

•Mike Candrea: "He grieved his wife's death, now U.S. softball coach must carry on," Elizabeth Merrill, ESPN.com 19 June 2008. Candrea's career highlights were compiled from the Arizona University website, the NCAA Softball Records Book and USA Softball Olympic Team Guides.

•Ralph Raymond: Dot Richardson, *Living The Dream*, Kensington, 1996; Paul Della Valle, "Ralph Raymond: The Winningest Coach That Ever Was," *Worcester Magazine*, 1 September 1993. Ralph Raymond's career highlights were compiled from the Connecticut Brakettes Team Guide, 2006, USA Softball Olympic Team Guides and the ASA National Softball Hall of Fame website.

•Joan Joyce: Dave Scheiber, "Joan Joyce; the best Ted Williams ever faced," ESPNW.com, 5 August, 2011. Joan Joyce's highlights were compiled from the Florida Atlanta University website, the ASA National Softball Hall of Fame website, Connecticut Brakettes Team Guide, 2006, and souvenir programs of the Connecticut Falcons.

•Sharron Backus: Sharron Backus' career highlights were compiled from the UCLA website, Connecticut Brakettes Team Guide, 2006, and the ASA National Softball Hall of Fame website.

•Sue Enquist: Sue Enquist career statistics were compiled from the UCLA website, Connecticut Brakettes Team Guide, 2006, and Enquist's website.sueenquist.com/home.html

•Carol Spanks: Carol Spanks' career highlights were compiled from the ASA National Softball Hall of Fame website, NFCA Hall of Fame, and Lionettes souvenir programs.

•Margie Wright: Margie Wright's career highlights were compiled from the Fresno State University website, and USA Softball Team Guides.

•Judi Garman: Judi Garman's career highlights were compiled from the Cal State Fullerton website, NCAA Softball Records Book, and the 2006 Women's College World Series Record Book.

•Cindy Bristow: Peggy Hesketh, "Girls of Summer," Orange, Calif. Independent, 3 February 1994, 1, 4. Cindy Bristow's career highlights were compiled from the Softball Excellence website, Cal Poly Pomona Team Guides and Orange Lionettes Team Yearbooks.

•Chapter 20 Information was compiled from the NCAA Softball Records Book and the ASA Hall of Fame website.

INDEX OF NAMES

INDEX OF NAMES

Photo Credits

USA Softball: pages xvi, 22, 32, 51, 52, 61, 62, 72, 108, 118 and 127; Texas A&M Sports Information: pages 84 and 97; UCLA Sports Information: pages 2, 11, 42, 140, 149 and 150; Stormy Irwin: pages 160, 169 and 204; Cindy Bristow, pages 192, 202 and 203; Oklahoma State University Sports Information: page 12; ESPN: page 21; Debbie Doom, page 98; Fresno State Sports Information: page 179; Judi Garman: pages 180 and 191; University of Tennessee Media Relations, page 71

Color section photo credits: USA Softball: Lisa Fernandez, Michele Smith, Cat Osterman, Jennie Finch, Dr. Dot Richardson, Monica Abbott and Mike Candrea; UCLA Sports Information: Natasha Watley, Stacey Nuveman, Sue Enquist and Debbie Doom; Fresno State Sports Information: Margie Wright; Joan Chandler: Joan Joyce; Texas A&M Sports Information: Shawn Andaya; Stormy Irwin: Carol Spanks; Judi Garman: Judi Garman; Cindy Bristow: Cindy Bristow; cover picture of softball courtesy Sarah Clarfield

Cover photo credits: Lisa Fernandez (UCLA Sports Information); Michele Smith (OSU Sports Information); Cat Osterman (USA Softball); Natasha Watley (USA Softball); Stacey Nuveman (UCLA Sports Information); Jennie Finch (USA Softball); Monica Abbott (USA Softball); Dot Richardson (USA Softball); Shawn Andaya (Texas A&M Sports Information); Debbie Doom (UCLA Sports Information); Mike Candrea (USA Softball); Joan Joyce (Florida Atlanta Sports Information); Sharron Backus (UCLA Sports Information); Sue Enquist (UCLA Sports Information); Carol Spanks (Stormy Irwin); Margie Wright (Fresno State Sports Information); Ralph Raymond (USA Softball); Judi Garman (Judi Garman); Cindy Bristow (Cindy Bristow)

ABOUT THE AUTHORS

BILL PLUMMER III

A 1973 graduate of Indiana University, Bloomington, Indiana, Bill Plummer III has been involved in softball for more than four decades. During his career, he served as a sports writer and a baseball scout, and for 30 years was a fixture at the ASA National Office in Oklahoma City as the communications coordinator, manager of the ASA National Softball Hall of Fame and historian.

In addition, Plummer also served as the editor of the ASA official newsletter, The Inside Pitch, and as the Trade Show Manager. He has written widely about the sport and has contributed to 13 books. In 2009, he authored *The Game America Plays: Celebrating 75 years of the Amateur Softball Association.*

He has been elected to five Halls of Fame, including the ASA National Softball Hall of Fame plus state Halls of Fame in Oklahoma, Indiana, Tidewater and New York State. In 1996, he served as the Information Manager for ACOG for the debut of softball in the Olympics.

Although he retired from the ASA in 2009, Plummer is still very involved in the sport, currently writing a column for the Lowe's CLASS softball winner each year and serving on its Selection Committee. He also produces newsletters for the ASA's in Texas and Tennessee and on occasion writes about different events at the ASA Hall of Fame Stadium, including being a stringer for the AP covering the NCAA Women's College World Series.

A native of Syracuse, New York, Plummer now lives in Oklahomas City, Oklahoma.

STEVEN CLARFIELD, PH.D.

Steven Clarfield, Ph. D., has been a practicing clinical and community psychologist since 1972 and has worked with public and private businesses since 1980. He maintains a private practice in Manalapan, N.J. where he works with individuals and families. Dr. Clarfield has consulted to multinational businesses, government agencies and for profit and non-profit corporations in areas related to team building, relationship enhancement and quality of life improvement.

At the age of 15, Steve began pitching in men's industrial and club team leagues. At 17 he began playing in interstate tournaments. During the period 1964-1972 he took a hiatus from competitive interstate softball to pursue a psychology doctorate degree and returned in 1973 to play a local N.J. fast pitch schedule. Between 1974 and 1989 he returned to a full interstate schedule playing in ASA sanctioned "AA" and "A"tournaments, state championships, regional qualifiers and national qualifiers.

Steve lives in Morganville with his wife of 26 years, Patricia. He has five children, Amanda, Julie, Joseph, Sarah and David and three grandchildren, Ryan, Elizabeth and Taylor. The "Best of the Best" is his most recent book since *Ty Stofflet, Softball's Lefty Legend* was published in 2004.